A PAULINE THEOLOGY
OF
CHARISMATA

Siegfried S. Schatzmann

HENDRICKSON
PUBLISHERS
PEABODY, MASSACHUSETTS 01961-3473

To Madi, my spouse,
to Myriam, my daughter,
and to David and Marcel, my sons,
joint-heirs with Christ.

ISBN 0-913573-45-0

Table of Contents

PREFACE   v

ABBREVIATIONS   viii

1. THE TERM "CHARISMA"   1

   Etymology   1
   Usage   4
   Synonyms   5
   Definition   7
   Summary   10

2. THE EXEGETICAL PERSPECTIVES OF CHARISMATA   14

   Romans 1:11   14
   Romans 5:15, 16   15
   Romans 6:23   17
   Romans 11:29   18
   Romans 12:6–8   19
   1 Corinthians 1:7   26
   1 Corinthians 7:7   28
   1 Corinthians 12–14   29
     The Corinthian Situation   30
     The Christological Test of Spiritual Giftedness, 12:1–3   31
     The Fundamental Character of Gifts, 12:4–6   34
     The Lists of Χαρίσματα, 12:8–10, 28, 29–30   35
     The Functional Purpose of Gifts, 12:12–27   46
     The Realm of the Gifts' Operation, 1 Cor 13   47
   2 Corinthians 1:11   48
   1 Timothy 4:14, 2 Timothy 1:6   49
   Summary   50

3. CHARISMATA AS THE CHURCH'S EQUIPMENT
FOR SERVICE   66

Individual and Corporate Aspects   67
Unity and Diversity of Charismata   70
Grace Endowment or Natural Talent   73
Permanence or Temporariness of Charismata   77
Summary   80

4. CHARISMATA AS MINISTERIAL FUNCTION   83

Equation of Charismata with Offices   84
Charismata as Ministry in Evangelism and Missions   87
Charismata for the World   89
Summary   90

5. CHARISMATA AS EXPRESSION OF AUTHORITY   94

The Equation of Charisma and Authority—Its Basis   95
The Scope of Charismata and Authority in the Church   97
The Manipulative Tendencies of Charismatic Authority   99
Summary   99

CONCLUSIONS   101

BIBLIOGRAPHY   104

INDEX OF AUTHORS   113

INDEX OF SCRIPTURE REFERENCES   115

Preface

The following study was originally submitted as my doctoral dissertation for the Ph.D. degree at Southwestern Baptist Theological Seminary in 1981. It was then presented under the title "The Pauline Concept of Charismata in the Light of Recent Critical Literature." In the fall of 1985 I had the pleasure of meeting Dr. Ben Aker, Executive Editor of Hendrickson Publishers, who read the manuscript and initiated its publication. While the content of the study has basically been left untouched, German and French quotations have either been translated into English or they were eliminated, if such excision did not impair the intended meaning. Since the major concern of this project was exegetical, and since exegesis must necessarily precede and inform theological discussion, the new title seems quite appropriate.

The need for an exegetical study of charismatic endowment arises for several reasons. One, the contemporary charismatic movement has contributed much to a renewed interest in the relevance of charismatic experience, both for the individual Christian and for the churches. As a result, writers from within the renewal movement have tended to be experientially oriented in their treatment of charismatic endowment and ministry. In this pursuit, the Pauline materials have been used for purposes of legitimizing experiential categories without consideration for the most important task of submitting such experience to the test of the biblical text and of its exegesis.

Two, until the rise of the charismatic renewal, the scholarly world treated the Pauline perspective on charismata rather nonchalantly as a theological category. Either these gifts were subsumed under the discussion of church offices or they were considered passé. But with the phenomenal growth of the classical Pentecostal churches and with the even more remarkable expansion of the charismatic movement, the lethargy has been replaced by a sense of acute need to find adequate answers for the phenomena encountered. In some cases, the scholarly position has been one of simply "digging in"; that is, traditional positions have been maintained with renewed vigor. But in general, students of Paul's writings have demonstrated a willingness to reexamine former positions in the light of experiential claims in order to arrive at more adequate interpretive and theological positions.

Three, particularly in the 1970s, the number of critical treatments of the Pauline concept of charismata has mushroomed in comparison to the former dearth of material (or interest). In many cases, however, the theological categories, and particularly the exegetical perspectives, appear to be influenced by ecclesiastical traditions and presuppositions, so that the results follow predictable lines.

It is my conviction that our primary task is to interpret the Pauline materials on charismata exegetically in order to arrive at a sound theological basis. Consequently, after an introductory first chapter dealing with the term "charisma" itself, the primary attention will be given to an exegesis of the relevant passages of those letters in which the Apostle Paul used the term. Therefore, the works consulted in the exegesis proper will necessarily exceed the general time frame of the decade 1970–1980. The literature incorporated in the other chapters adheres more closely to this self-imposed time frame.

The exegetical approach seems best to establish a working basis for discussion. In the succeeding chapters some of the key issues concerning charismata will be discussed. Each of those chapters will also reexamine certain interpretive points raised in the exegesis, but from the perspective of the particular issue.

I am gratefully indebted to my advisor in doctoral studies, Professor Dr. Jack W. MacGorman, for his influence upon me, as well as for his willingness to devote countless hours to the fruitful exchange of salient points of interpretation during my years of residence at Southwestern. His expertise and guidance in the preparation of the original dissertation made the project enjoyable.

I am further indebted to the Committee of the Doctor of Philosophy Degree of the School of Theology of Southwestern Baptist Theological Seminary for their kind permission to publish this study through Hendrickson Publishers.

A sincere note of appreciation is also in order for Dr. Ben Aker's initiation and Mr. Stephen Hendrickson's diligent execution of the publication process. The congenial help of Mr. Patrick Alexander, Associate Editor, has facilitated the revision of the manuscript greatly. I am also grateful to Mrs. Melanie Tollett for her meticulous typing of the final draft of the manuscript, as well as to Mr. James Pair, my assistant in the spring semester of 1986, for preparing the indices. Above all else, *soli Deo gloria*.

Tulsa, Oklahoma,
March 1986

Abbreviations

AB	The Anchor Bible
adj.	adjective
AnBib	Analecta Biblica
AV	Authorized Version
BAGD	Bauer, Arndt, Gingrich, and Danker, *A Greek-English Lexicon of the New Testament and Other Early Christian Literature*
BHT	Beiträge zur historischen Theologie
BS	*Bibliotheca Sacra*
BTB	*Biblical Theology Bulletin*
BWANT	Beiträge zur Wissenschaft vom Alten und Neuen Testament
BZ	*Biblische Zeitschrift*
CGTC	Cambridge Greek Testament Commentaries
ch(s)	chapter(s)
cod.	codex
CTM	*Concordia Theological Monthly*
dat.	dative
EBib	Études Bibliques
ET	English Translation
EvQ	*Evangelical Quarterly*
ExpGT	*Expositor's Greek Testament, ed. W. R. Nicoll*
ExpT	*Expository Times*
FS	Festschrift
gen.	genitive
Gk	Greek
GNC	Good News Commentary
HNT	Handbuch zum Neuen Testament
HNTC	Harper's New Testament Commentaries
HTKNT	Herder's theologischer Kommentar zum Neuen Testament
IB	Interpreter's Bible, 12 vols.
ICC	International Critical Commentary

impv(s).	imperative(s)
infin.	infinitive
JR	*Journal of Religion*
JTS	*Journal of Theological Studies*
KEKNT	Kritisch-Exegetischer Kommentar über das Neue Testament
LXX	Septuagint
masc.	masculine
MNTC	Moffatt New Testament Commentary
MSS	manuscripts
n.	note
NASB	New American Standard Bible
NCeB	The New Century Bible Commentary
NEB	New English Bible
neut.	neuter
NICNT	New International Commentary of the New Testament
NIDNTT	*New International Dictionary of New Testament Theology*, ed. C. Brown
NIV	New International Version
NT	New Testament
NTD	Das Neue Testament Deutsch
NTS	*New Testament Studies*
NTSMS	New Testament Studies Monograph Series
OT	Old Testament
p.c.	and a few others (*pauci*)
pass.	passive
pl.	plural
pres.	present (tense)
pron.	pronoun
pt.	part
RBV	Revised Berkeley Version
repr.	reprint
RSV	Revised Standard Version
sg.	singular
SWJT	*Southwestern Journal of Theology*
syn.	synonymous
TDNT	*Theological Dictionary of the New Testament*, eds. G. Kittel and G. Friedrich
THKNT	Theologischer Handkommentar zum Neuen Testament
TLZ	*Theologische Literaturzeitung*
Tyn	Tyndale New Testament Commentaries

TZ	*Theologische Zeitschrift*
USQR	*Union Seminary Quarterly Review*
v/vv	verse(s)
WC	Westminster Commentaries
WPC	Westminster Pelican Commentaries
WS	Wuppertaler Studienbibel
ZTK	*Zeitschrift für Theologie und Kirche*

1
The Term "Charisma"

MANY RECENT TREATMENTS of "charismata," or aspects of them, have hinged upon theological categorizations and presuppositions. Often these have also borne the marks of differing denominational perspectives. Such vested interests, imperceptibly or consciously, become the critical hermeneutical factor, subordinating what the texts say to secondary significance. This study seeks to reverse that process. Therefore, chapter I focuses on the term "charisma" itself. The primary question to be asked is: What factors contributed to the distinctiveness of Paul's concept of "charismata"? Four possible factors deserve a close look for potential answers: (I) Basic to an in-depth study is an etymological investigation. (2) Related to that is a study of the term's usage. (3) Also necessary is a study of the term's synonyms, as witnessed in the Pauline writings. (4) The fourth factor concerns a definition of the term, to ascertain the meaning of "charismata."

ETYMOLOGY

In order to understand how the word received its distinctiveness, one must not look for cause in the current or popular usage. Such an attempt would be fruitless; for it only points to a watering down of the term's meaning in secular vocabulary. The popular conception of "charisma" began with the German sociologist Max Weber, who sought to bring Pauline ideas of leadership to bear upon his contemporaries. However, there exists little parallelism between popular usage and the term's meaning as seen in the NT.[1] In fact, to argue back to Paul from Weber's contemporary usage is only to end up in a terminological cul-de-sac. More appropriate is to explore the etymology of the concept.

Χάρισμα is derived from the root word χάρις. Whereas the former is used sparingly, the latter occurs profusely both in secular Greek literature and in the NT.[2] Χάρις, in the Pauline letters generally translated as "grace," and χάρισμα, the unique NT term for "gift," develop from the stem χαρ-.[3] "Grace" is probably Paul's most fundamental concept by which he expresses the event of salvation. It is crucial to understand, therefore, that "grace" does not, for Paul, convey the notion of God's disposition or attitude towards mankind but rather God's gracious "act." Rudolf Bultmann appropriately summarizes the foundational character of χάρις in Paul as "God's eschatological deed."[4] Paul's theology is thus appropriately described as "charitocentric";[5] χάρις denotes God's "fundamental gift of salvation" to humanity.[6] By no means must this be construed to mean that Paul considered "grace" as God's generous act in the past only. Even a cursory study of such passages as Rom 3:24, 5:15, and Eph 2:5, 8, shows that grace, as God's eschatological event in Christ, is experienced in the present and also transforms and characterizes existence in the present. This understanding of χάρις, then, leads to its correlate, χάρισμα. Yet, the further probing into the significance of the relatedness of these terms must await the exegesis of Rom 5:15, 16, and of 6:23.

Another possible root for χάρισμα is the verb χαρίζομαι. But it seems evident that the latter is itself based on the noun χάρισμα—and, as such, does not have the precise sense of the noun. While its basic sense is "to give" or "to act kindly" (e.g. Gal 3:18), it denotes rather frequently, "to forgive" (2 Cor 2:7, 10; 12:13; Eph 4:32). The noun χάρισμα can be understood as a verbal noun; i.e., a verbal construct employing the suffix -μα.[7] The type of noun ending in -μα generally designates the result of an act or activity. The noun χάρισμα would thus denote the "concrete result of bestowal."[8] But since the more basic noun χάρις conveys the same, the argument for etymological nuances tends to become circular.

The Pauline distinctiveness of "charisma" also implies that Paul is not indebted to the OT for it. In fact, the term occurs only twice in the LXX, and then only in variant readings of the deuterocanonical Ecclesiasticus (Sirach). In ch 7:33 χάρισμα is attested only in Codex Sinaiticus, whereas the other manuscripts use χάρις: "Give graciously to all the living, and withold not *kindness* from the dead."

In Eccl 38:30 the term is used in the Codex Vaticanus[9] to denote "a lovely work" which the potter endeavors to create. It is noteworthy that in both instances χάρισμα does not involve God but describes a favor, an event or attitude, between human beings or between man and his handiwork. Considering the almost nonexistent usage of charisma in the

LXX, coupled with the total absence of a Hebrew equivalent, it is difficult to conceive that Paul could have borrowed the term from his acquaintance with the LXX.[10] Theodotion's translation of *hesed* as χάρισμα in Ps 30:22,[11] instead of ἔλεος, following the LXX, does not provide further clues concerning the source of Paul's use of the term. Again the evidence is too weak to argue from Theodotion's usage to Paul's.

Whereas the concept is missing altogether in Josephus, Philo's two-fold usage of χάρισμα θεοῦ in *Legum Allegoria* 3.78 is questionable, at best,[12] and may represent a late reading. More significant may be Philo's synonymous usage of χάρισμα with χάρις in the first instance and with δωρεά and ἐνεργεσία in the second. But since the passage is suspect of representing a later interpolation, one might postulate the possibility of a Pauline reflection upon Philo's editor. Thus, Siegfried Schulz categorically classified all of the citations listed as "late variants as far as textual criticism is concerned."[13] Further, the occurrence of the term in the Sibylline Oracles (2:54) is also considered a late addition to the document.[14]

In secular Greek the term does not fare any better. The best attested and earliest evidence comes from the sophist Alciphron. But this occurrence is irrelevant for etymological purposes because of its second century AD date. The next best examples from secular Greek come from several papyri of later Christian centuries. They are no longer pertinent to this study.[15]

With reference to post-apostolic Greek writings, charisma also occurs in several of the writings of the apostolic fathers (Did 1:5; Ign Eph 17:2; Ign Pol 2:2; Ign Smyrn 9:2 [2x]; 1 Clem 38:1). But with the probable exception of Did 1:5, these references bear the marks of Pauline influence.[16]

Summarizing the etymological findings, then, two observations can be made with a fair degree of certainty. One, the term χάρισμα was in circulation in secular, and perhaps in cultic, language before Paul. Nevertheless, the scant evidence also points to an equally sparse usage. Two, more than any other Pauline concept, χάρισμα received its terminological significance from the Apostle Paul. This observation necessarily raises an additional question. If the term received its distinctiveness through the Apostle Paul, what provided the impetus for this elevation to significance?

USAGE

Even in the NT χάρισμα is a relatively rare word, occurring only seventeen times. With the exception of 1 Pet 4:10, all the references are found in the Pauline corpus.[17] Of the sixteen citations in Paul, six occur in Romans (1:11; 5:15, 16; 6:23; 11:29; 12:6) and seven in 1 Corinthians (1:7; 7:7; 12:4, 9, 28, 30, 31). The remaining three references are found in 2 Cor 1:11, 1 Tim 4:14, and 2 Tim 1:6. While it is improbable that Paul coined the word, he was certainly the first to give the term its distinctive significance. However, to speak of distinctive significance is not warranty to regard the term χάρισμα as a fully developed *terminus technicus*,[18] especially when the term is conspicuous by its rarity. At best one might affirm that, for Paul, the term became a technical one in Romans and in 1 Corinthians.

Did Paul himself introduce the term to the vocabulary of the Christian community, or was the church familiar with it before Paul so that he may have used an already current expression? No evidence can be adduced in support of the latter. Even the frequent usage in 1 Corinthians, chronologically the first Pauline letter in which it appears,[19] does not permit the conclusion that the Corinthians had used χάρισμα as their term. The exegesis to follow will show that their term was πνευματικά, whereas Paul seems to have introduced χάρισμα[τα] as an apostolic corrective.[20] The term's significance is, therefore, uniquely Paul's contribution, which came to fruition through his own encounter with Christ. James D. G. Dunn observed this point clearly, noting that "the main influence determining Paul's choice of the word is his own experience, the creative experiences which it describes."[21]

The distinctiveness of the term is also underscored by the range and nuances of its meaning. Paul used the concept with remarkable versatility, considering that it appears only fourteen times in the Corinthian and Roman correspondences. The purpose of the following outline of the varied usage is merely to point out the term's distinctiveness, and will be dealt with in greater detail in chapter 2.

First, Paul employed the term in a "nontechnical," general sense. Typically, χάρισμα here overlaps considerably with χάρις, as in Rom 5:15, 16, as well as in 6:23, though here without the use of the latter term, and it constitutes the broadest range of meaning. It embraces both the gracious act of God in Jesus Christ and the all-inclusive result of that act with reference to the believer. Paul declares succinctly: "the free gift (χάρισμα) of God is eternal life in Christ Jesus" (Rom 6:23, RSV).

Second, twice the term is used for specific gifts given to the believer. In 1 Cor 7:7, speaking of celibacy, Paul individualizes χάρισμα: "Each man has his own gift from God."[22] The reference in 2 Cor 1:11 speaks of charisma as the divine favor granted in rescuing Paul from a perilous situation. It is also possible, of course, to assign 1 Cor 7:7 to the third category below, especially if it can be shown that the purpose of celibacy is none other than that of the other manifestations of grace in 1 Cor 12:8-10 and Rom 12:6-8, namely the οἰκοδομή of the church. Likewise, 2 Cor 1:11 could be included in the category of the term's nontechnical use.[23]

Third, most frequently the term denotes a manifestation of grace within the community of believers. In Rom 11:29 the focus is upon God's gracious act towards Israel, his OT people whose election is established in their gift and calling. The primary passages, Rom 12:6–8 and 1 Cor 12–14, reflect the particular gifts, as a result of God's grace, for the upbuilding of the body of Christ. Χάρισμα receives even greater distinctiveness through its plural forms, as well as through the unique, divine key of distribution.[24] The two occurrences in Rom 1:11 and 1 Cor 1:7 fall under the same category.

If 1 Tim 4:14 and 2 Tim 1:6 are taken into consideration, a fourth nuance in usage might become necessary, namely one focusing upon the institutional significance. The receiving of a charisma under the laying on of hands is characteristic only in the Pastoral Letters and may, therefore, reflect a later development which is not yet noticeable in the earlier Pauline writings. What Paul may have in mind here could be described as charismatic office.

The term's distinctiveness, therefore, comes to light both in its adaptability to general and particular usage and in its ability to express thematic unity (grace) and diversity (gifts). Χάρισμα is unquestionably the term which Paul made distinctive and important. And yet, he did not monopolize it; rather, he demonstrated amazing linguistic agility by using other terms with virtually synonymous meaning. Attention will now be given to these.

SYNONYMS

For Paul, distinctiveness did not mean exclusiveness. He used synonyms both in verbal and in substantival forms. Just as χαρίζομαι expresses the general action of giving, so δίδωμι denotes the same basic action.²⁵ In the NT the subject of the verb is frequently God, Jesus, or the Holy Spirit who bestows blessings on humans.

The noun forms occur with equal variety. In Eph 4:8 Paul states, "He [Christ] gave gifts [δώματα] to men"; and in 4:7 the apostle introduces this quote with the statement, "But to each of us grace [χάρις] has been given [ἐδόθη] according to the measure of the gift [δωρεᾶς] of Christ." In Rom 5:15 δωρεά is used interchangeably with χάρισμα, while in 5:16 Paul further parallels δώρημα with χάρισμα. And in Eph 2:8 the use of δῶρον to underscore the grace character of salvation carries the same basic thrust. In 1 Cor 12:4–6 the plural χαρίσματα is also paralleled by the terms διακονίαι and ἐνεργήματα.²⁶ Such profusion and variety of parallel terms expressing "gifts" compel John Koenig to speak of "the language of giftedness" which confronts us "with an embarrassment of riches."²⁷

To the "language of giftedness" also belongs the noun τὰ πνευματικά which Paul uses twice in a plural form in 1 Cor 12:1 and 14:1. No other word has stirred as passionate a debate in the discussion of spiritual gifts. The question of relationship between πνευματικά and χαρίσματα seems to give rise to ever new discussion. Are they synonymous or not? One of three positions is generally maintained. One, πνευματικά is completely synonymous because χάρις and πνεῦμα are also interchangeable.²⁸ Thus πνευματικά stands "for the totality of the gifts of the Spirit."²⁹

Two, there is qualified synonymity between the two terms. In this case, parallelism is predicated either upon the contextual relationship³⁰ or upon the function of the πνευματικά, namely upon their upbuilding of the church and upon the acclamation "Jesus is Lord."³¹ To the extent that the πνευματικά/χαρίσματα do not fulfill these functions in the Corinthian context, Paul is critical of their use; hence his stress of grace as the basis for the gifts of the Spirit. The disorder in the Corinthian church may indeed have been directly linked to the lack of understanding life in the Spirit as a charisma.³² D. W. B. Robinson approves qualified synonymity on the basis of 14:1, but adds that πνευματικά is not the general term for spiritual gifts. Paul introduced the term "charismata" intentionally in chs 12–14 to broaden the basis for what the Corinthians considered to be πνευματικά only. Thus "charismata" emerges as the Pauline corrective, and the parallelism must be sought in Paul's intended use of the concepts. It is quite possible, therefore, that the Corinthians regarded πνευματικά as their *terminus technicus*.³³

Three, the supposed synonymity does not exist. E. Earle Ellis has argued extensively that "the term is not equivalent to the more general χαρίσματα, although it may be identified with the 'greater charisms' (Rom 1:11; 1 Cor 14:1, 12:31)." He maintains that in 1 Cor 12−14 πνευματικά is used in a more restricted sense of prophetic gifts of inspired speech and discernment.[34] But the argument does not convince with reference to 14:1 (ζηλοῦτε δὲ τὰ πνευματικά) in which the parallelism with 12:31 (ζηλοῦτε δὲ τὰ χαρίσματα [τὰ μείζονα]) is unmistakable.

To deny any and all parallelism, therefore, not only does injustice to the text in its context, but seems to serve the presuppositional notion that πνευματικά could mean nothing more than "inspired utterance." The same applies to the view that the synonymity is absolute. Qualified interchangeability best characterizes Paul's use of the terms. Further discussion on the issue will have to be held pending the investigation of the context of 1 Cor 12−14. It is necessary now to return to the term "charismata" itself and to attempt a provisional definition.

DEFINITION

In matters of etymology there exists considerable agreement: in the scarcity of the term in secular and religious literature outside of Paul, χάρισμα received its distinctiveness through the Apostle Paul himself. And a certain consensus is also noticeable regarding Paul's free usage of synonymous terms. But definitional impressions and attempts have defied the quest for consensus thus far. The question is forced upon every serious student of the Pauline materials: Is it possible at all to define χαρίσματα with one simple phrase while incorporating the multiple concerns Paul seemed to have invested in the term? Even a cursory survey of the pertinent critical literature dispels that naive hope. There is no such thing as an "on-line definition for a complex concept." The number and variety of definitions seem to increase commensurate with new publications on the subject.

Perhaps a feasible approach consists of the gathering of definitional categories and their subsequent synthesis into a compound definition. Recent studies call for the following categories to be considered: (1) forms of the Käsemannian "concrete expression of grace"; (2) those of experiential nature; (3) those of the idealistic-naturalistic bent; (4) dogmatic-institutional versions; and (5) certain multiplex attempts.

Concrete Expression of Grace

Ernst Käsemann defines charisma as "individuation of grace, our personal participation in the *Pneuma*, and the concretion of our Christian calling."[35] Accordingly, he emphasizes the grace aspect of justification and its outworking in the community of faith. In his *Commentary on Romans*, Käsemann moves beyond his rather broad definition of χαρίσματα as "concrete forms of charis" and includes the aspect of service: "Charisma is the πνευματικόν taken into the service of Christ."[36] John Goldingay's definition appears to bear the marks of Käsemann's rendering: "Charisma is God's grace finding particular and concrete actualisation."[37] Schulz has effectively refined Käsemann's concerns and added his own insights. He suggests: "Charisma, according to Paul, is first of all gift, present, apportioning, then manifestation, concretion and individuation of one and the same Spirit, the outworking of grace as power and, finally, it is appointment to service to one's neighbour, including the enemy. . . ."[38]

Experiential

The experience of grace constitutes an important facet in understanding charismata. Although this aspect by no means exhausts the meaning of the term in Pauline usage, it must be considered without apology. James Dunn has undoubtedly served us well by pointing out that charisma always has the character of an event; as such it is "the experience of grace and power in a *particular instance and only for that instance*."[39] God's gifts to the redeemed take on meaning only in the event of their being experienced; without their being experienced they remain abstractions and theological formulae. On the other hand, one must guard against existential exclusiveness in defining charismata merely as "public expressions of personal experience."[40] The particularity of the experience of charismata depends largely upon the context in which Paul used the term in the respective passages, as Duane Priebe has shown.[41]

Idealistic-Naturalistic

While F. C. Baur's idealistic interpretation of charismata[42] has long been dismissed as untenable by most students of Pauline writings, it tends to resurface, with modifications, in those who define charisma as natural talent drawn into divine service. The German charismatic Arnold Bittlinger has consistently maintained that "everything, however ordinary or extraordinary, can be made use of by God for the neighbour's or the world's salvation, and thereby becomes a charism."[43] Elsewhere he defines thus: "A gift is manifested when being set free by the Holy Spirit, my natural endowments blossom forth glorifying Christ and building up His church."[44] What causes concern here is the de facto definition of all charismata as natural or ordinary abilities and vice versa. One cannot avoid the suspicion that a deliberate attempt is made to find a working formula for the profound realization that "all Christians are charismatic, or they are not Christians at all."[45] By this observation alone the question of how the nature of charismata is to be understood is not answered adequately, however; and more will have to be said in chapter 3. Suffice it to reiterate that defining charismata under exclusively naturalistic categories is to resurrect Baur's idealistic view.

Dogmatic-Institutional

Karl Rahner, who has consistently approached exegetical and theological questions from the Catholic ecclesiastical stance, defines charisma strictly within dogmatic parameters. When he asserts that charisma denotes an experience of the Spirit which is, as such, the "grace-filled, divinising gift of God to justified mankind," Rahner defines strictly according to the dogma of the church.[46] Consequently, he understands by "charismatic," "what is in contradistinction to what is purely institutional, administered by men, subject to calculation and expressible in laws and rules."[47] Granted the special interests of the dogmatic theologian, it does not suffice simply to juxtapose charisma and institution. Nor does the Pauline perspective allow the church to inform charismata and confine them to its various predetermined molds. The opposite is needed. The Pauline paraenesis on the gifts of the Spirit needs to inform and transform the institution and its dogmas. In other words, a definition of charisma must first of all reflect exegetical insights, not theological and dogmatic formulations of the institution.

Multiplex

Χαρίσματα, even for Paul, appears to have been a complex concept with a wide range of application. Recent research on the subject reflects the multifacetedness and the resultant difficulty of concise definition. Multiplex definitions seek to incorporate the primary emphases which Paul seems to have placed in the different contexts of the Corinthian and Roman correspondences. Inevitably, this generates not only definitions comprised of multiplex strands of truth, but it also gives rise to multiple combinations in the wording and placing of these strands. In order to demonstrate this, a sampling of recent definitions follows.

John Koenig defines: "The apostle Paul especially uses it (charismata) to describe gifts of God (not always spectacular) that differentiate believing individuals from one another for the purpose of enhancing their mutual service."[48] Dunn's discussion on matters of definition could be summarized thus: "Charisma can only be understood as a particular expression of charis, as the gracious activity of God through a man . . . for others; charisma is the experience of grace given."[49] Hasenhüttl suggests: "Charisma is the specific and concrete calling, encompassing time and eternity, which is received through the salvation event, finds its realization in the community, which it constitutes and continually builds up, and lovingly serves fellowman."[50]

Perhaps the laboriousness of the definitions is in direct proportion to the scant usage in the NT and to the variety of meanings Paul attached to the term charisma. Attempts at definition will almost certainly continue to vary greatly. And yet, any definition to be considered ought to say something about its etymological moorings, about the divine and human aspects in its experience, and about the function or purpose of charisma. However, this task will be undertaken only after the exegesis, whose results also need to inform definitional endeavors. For the moment, it suffices to note that the broad spectrum of definitions only underscores the distinctiveness of the term in Paul's usage.

SUMMARY

Χάρισμα as a Pauline concept can only be characterized as distinctive. Etymologically it receives its distinctiveness as a derivative of the root word χάρις, and is rendered conspicuous by the scarcity of the term in Judaic and secular Greek writings as well as in the patristic literature. In terms of Pauline usage, the noun χάρισμα becomes distinctive by the wide range of meaning which the apostle invests in it. The ease which Paul demonstrates in employing synonymous expressions such as δωρεά, δώρημα, δώματα, and even χάρις, further enhances the uniqueness of χάρισμα as Paul's preferred term for giftedness. Then, the complex task of defining χάρισμα as a multifaceted concept denotes distinctiveness. Considering the evidence, one may be confronted with a unique example of the apostle's linguistic ability. There exists ample evidence that Paul gave new meaning to popular Greek concepts used in the

Hellenistic environment. But the distinctiveness he bestowed upon the term—an otherwise little-known Greek concept—may indeed be unique. With that distinctiveness in mind, the exegesis of Pauline texts containing the term must be undertaken next.

NOTES

1. He defines "charisma" as "extraordinary quality of a person." Max Weber, "Die Wirtschaftsethik der Weltreligionen," in *Gesammelte Aufsätze zur Religionssoziologie*, 5th ed. (Tübingen: J. C. B. Mohr [Paul Siebeck], 1963), 1:268. He recognizes its actual usage and *Sitz im Leben* in Paul, but then proceeds to use the term in an entirely non-Pauline manner.

2. See the relevant discussions in the *TDNT* 9:372–76; *NIDNTT* 2:118.

3. J. Koenig, *Charismata: God's Gifts for God's People*, in *Biblical Perspectives on Current Issues*, ed. H. C. Kee (Philadelphia: Westminster, 1978), 54. Similarly, the NT terms "joy" (χάρα) and "thanks" (εὐχαριστία) are based on the same stem.

4. R. Bultmann, *Theology of the New Testament*, transl. K. Grobel (New York: Charles Scribner's Sons, 1951), 1:289; J. D. G. Dunn, *Jesus and the Spirit: A Study of the Religious and Charismatic Experiences of Jesus and the First Christians as Reflected in the New Testament* (Philadelphia: Westminster, 1975), 202–3.

5. So P. Bonnetain, *Dictionnaire de la Bible*, Supplément 3:1002, quoted by Dunn, *Jesus and the Spirit*, 409.

6. Ignace de LaPotterie, "Χάρις Paulinienne et χάρις Johannique," in *Jesus und Paulus*, FS W. G. Kümmel zum 70. Geburtstag, ed. E. Earle Ellis and Erich Grässer (Göttingen: Vandenhoeck & Ruprecht, 1975), 268–69. Similarly, D. J. Doughty, "The Priority of χάρις: An Investigation of the Theological Language of Paul," *NTS* 19 (1972–73): 176–79. But see S. Neill, *The Interpretation of the New Testament 1861–1961* (London: Oxford University Press, 1964), 189, who asserts that "Paul's doctrine of the Spirit is far more central and characteristic than his doctrine of justification by faith."

7. Conzelmann, *TDNT*, 9:402–3; G. Hasenhüttl, *Charisma: Ordnungsprinzip der Kirche* (Freiburg im Breisgau: Verlag Herder K. G., 1969), 104–5.

8. Hasenhüttl, *Charisma*, 104–5.

9. The other MSS use χρίσμα, which may indicate a scribal error on the part of a copyist of cod. Vaticanus (B).

10. Hasenhüttl, *Charisma*, 105; Conzelmann, *TDNT*, 9:403.

11. English and Hebrew, Ps 31:22.

12. E. Käsemann, "Amt und Gemeinde im Neuen Testament," in *Exegetische Versuche und Besinnungen*, vol. 1, 5th ed. (Göttingen: Vandenhoeck & Ruprecht, 1976); "Ministry and Community in the New Testament," *Essays on New Testament Themes*, transl. W. J. Montague (London: SCM, 1964), 64, n. 1.

13. S. Schulz, "Die Charismenlehre des Paulus. Bilanz der Probleme und Ergebnisse," in *Rechtfertigung*, FS Ernst Käsemann zum 70. Geburtstag, ed.

J. Friedrich, W. Pöhlmann, and P. Stuhlmacher (Tübingen: J. C. B. Mohr, and Göttingen: Vandenhoeck & Ruprecht, 1976), 445.

14. J. Geffcken, *Komposition und Entstehungszeit der Oracula Sibyllina* (Leipzig: J. C. Hinrichs, 1902), 52, cited by U. Brockhaus, *Charisma und Amt: Die Paulinische Charismenlehre auf dem Hintergrund der frühchristlichen Gemeindefunktionen*, 2nd ed. (Wuppertal: Theologischer Verlag Rolf Brockhaus, 1974), 128.

15. *TDNT*, 9:403.

16. Käsemann, "Ministry and Community," 64. R. A. N. Kydd offers a fine discussion of charismata in the patristic era in *Charismatic Gifts in the Early Church* (Peabody, MA: Hendrickson, 1984).

17. Conzelmann considers the Petrine usage as "merely an echo" of Paul, *TDNT*, 9:403; similarly, Brockhaus, *Charisma und Amt*, 129. But this may be too narrowly conceived; and it negates a priori the knowledge and usage of the term outside of Paul, however limited that usage may have been.

18. Against R. Banks, *Paul's Idea of Community: The Early House Churches in Their Historical Setting* (Grand Rapids: Eerdmans, 1978), 94.

19. On the priority of 1 Corinthians over Romans, see H. Conzelmann, *1 Corinthians*, transl. J. W. Leitch, bibliography and references by J. W. Dunkly, Hermeneia, ed. G. W. MacRae (Philadelphia: Fortress, 1975), 2–5. On the view that Romans has priority over 1 Corinthians, see J. R. Richards, "Romans and 1 Corinthians: Their Chronological Relationship and Comparative Dates," *NTS* 13 (10, 1966): 14–30; more recently, W. J. Hollenweger seems to have assumed this position in his *Conflict in Corinth and Memoirs of an Old Man. Two Stories that illuminate the way the Bible came to be written* (New York: Paulist, 1982).

20. Brockhaus, *Charisma und Amt*, 129–30.

21. Dunn, *Jesus and the Spirit*, 206.

22. Koenig, *Charismata*, 108, calls it "Paul's special gift."

23. So, Conzelmann, *1 Corinthians*, 208.

24. A. C. Piepkorn, "*Charisma* in the New Testament and the Apostolic Fathers," *CTM* 42 (6, 1971): 378–79.

25. In Rom 1:11 the compound verb μεταδίδωμι occurs in conjunction with χάρισμα, where the meaning is "to share," "to give a part of," or "to impart." See also Rom 12:6.

26. Koenig, *Charismata*, 54, incorporates "blessing," "abundance," "riches," "distribution," and "measure" as terms often denoting divine gifts, although these are not directly pertinent to this study. On δωρεά, cf. J. D. G. Dunn, "A Note on δωρεά," *ExpT* 81 (8, 1970): 349.

27. Koenig, *Charismata*, 54. Käsemann's suggestion that κλῆσις in Rom 11:29 is synonymous with χάρισμα is not automatically given. See exegesis on the above passage, "Ministry and Community," 64.

28. Bultmann, *Theology of the NT*, 1:155–56. According to Bultmann, Paul conceived of grace as spiritual power; e.g., 1 Cor 15:10 and 2 Cor 12:9.

29. *TDNT*, s.v. "πνεῦμα, πνευματικός," by E. Schweizer, 6:437.

30. E.g., Dunn, *Jesus and the Spirit*, 208; and "Spirit," *NIDNTT*, 3:707.

31. Doughty, "Priority of χάρις," 178–79.

32. Ibid., 179.

33. Schulz, "Die Charismenlehre des Paulus," 454.

34. E. E. Ellis, "Christ and Spirit in 1 Corinthians," in *Christ and Spirit in the New Testament. Studies in Honour of Charles Francis Digby Moule*, ed. B. Lindars and S. S. Smalley (Cambridge: Cambridge University Press, 1973), 274; and "Spiritual Gifts in the Pauline Community," *NTS* 20 (1, 1974): 128–29. Similarly, R. C. Oudersluys, "Charismatic Theology and the New Testament," *Reformed Review* 28 (Autumn 1974): 54.

35. Käsemann, "Ministry and Community," 80; *Commentary on Romans*, transl. and ed. G. W. Bromiley (Grand Rapids: Eerdmans, 1980), 333.

36. Käsemann, *Romans*, 333, 339.

37. J. Goldingay, *The Church and the Gifts of the Spirit*, Grove Booklets No. 7 (Bramcote Notts.: n.p., 1972), 5.

38. Schulz, "Die Charismenlehre des Paulus," 447. Similarly, J. Moltmann, *The Church in the Power of the Spirit. A Contribution to Messianic Ecclesiology*, transl. M. Kohl (New York: Harper & Row, 1977), 295.

39. Dunn, *Jesus and the Spirit*, 254, (italics are his). His insistence that charismatic experience be only for a particular instance probably needs to be understood in terms of event, and not in terms of time; otherwise, Paul's statement concerning Israel in Rom 11:29 loses much of its significance.

40. H. C. Kee, *Preface to "Charismata"*, by J. Koenig, 8.

41. D. A. Priebe, "Charismatic Gifts and Christian Existence in Paul," in *Gifts of the Spirit and the Body of Christ: Perspectives on the Charismatic Movement*, ed. J. E. Agrimson (Minneapolis: Augsburg, 1974), 20–21.

42. F. C. Baur, *Paul the Apostle of Jesus Christ, his Life and Work, his Epistles and his Doctrine. A Contribution to the Critical History of Primitive Christianity*, 2nd ed., ed. after the author's death by E. Zeller, transl. A. Menzies (London: Williams & Norgate, 1875), 2:172. Baur claims: "The charisms are originally nothing but the gifts and qualities which each man brings with him to Christianity; and these gifts and qualities are exalted into charisms because the Christian consciousness and life are founded on them, and reared on the materials which they bring, and moulded by the operation of the Spirit into their different individual forms."

43. A. Bittlinger, "Charismatic Renewal: An Opportunity for the Church," *The Ecumenical Review* 31 (7, 1979): 249.

44. A. Bittlinger, *Gifts and Graces: A Commentary on 1 Corinthians 12–14*, transl. H. Klassen (Grand Rapids: Eerdmans, 1967), 72.

45. W. J. Hollenweger, *The Pentecostals: The Charismatic Movement in the Churches*, transl. R. A. Wilson (Minneapolis: Augsburg, 1972), 429.

46. K. Rahner, *Theological Investigations, vol. 16, Experience of the Spirit: Source of Theology*, transl. D. Morland (New York: Seabury, 1979), 36.

47. K. Rahner, *The Spirit in the Church*, transl. J. Griffiths (New York: Seabury, 1979), 37.

48. Koenig, *Charismata*, 14.

49. Dunn, *Jesus and the Spirit*, 253–58. This is an attempt to gather the major strands of Dunn's definitions (for which he uses five pages) into a synthetic statement. It may, therefore, not accurately reflect Dunn's intended seminal concerns. This writer assumes responsibility for acting as editor. See also Dunn's article on πνεῦμα, *NIDNTT*, 3:702–3.

50. Hasenhüttl, *Charisma*, 238.

2
The Exegetical Perspectives of Charismata

IN KEEPING WITH THE PRESUPPOSITIONS stated earlier, all sixteen Pauline occurrences of the term χαρίσματα require exegetical attention. Observation and results will be gathered upon completion of the exegesis. The sequence of passages follows the canonical order.

ROMANS 1:11

In the course of expressing his desire to visit the Roman Christians as well, the Apostle Paul formulated the intent of such a visit as the imparting to them, or sharing among them, of "some spiritual gift." The curious use of the indefinite adjective τι does not shroud the statement in vagueness but allows Paul to leave open the possibilities for functioning among them with that gift (or those gifts) which he deemed most appropriate upon his arrival.[1] Any speculation as to what specific gift Paul may have had in mind is unprofitable.

Of greater interest appears to be the noun-adjective combination of χάρισμα πνευματικόν. This is the only occurrence of the term with a modifier. From this usage interpreters have drawn opposing conclusions. For some the necessity of πνευματικός to modify χάρισμα means that this Pauline concept is not as clear as it appears.[2] It might be more adequately rendered as "benefaction" or simply as "gift" or "present." For Daniel Fraikin, only the general translation of χάρισμα as "gift" represents Paul here because the adjective itself does not include the notion of "gift"; if it did, Paul would have stated a pure tautology.[3] The arbitrary distinction between "spiritual charisma" and "general (nonspiritual?) charisma" is a modern invention and, thus, totally foreign to Paul.[4]

For others, precisely the inclusion of πνευματικός serves to emphasize what is already implied in the noun charisma. Therefore, Paul could only have meant a "spiritual gift," analogous to his usage of the term in Rom 12:6 and in 1 Cor 12.[5] "Spiritual," in this case, does not qualify the otherwise general, unprecise noun, but it points to the source of the charisma, namely the Holy Spirit.[6]

In the context of vv 11b and 12, the purpose for this charismatic ministry was twofold. The members of the Roman community were to be strengthened and mutually encouraged in their faith.[7] Paul fully expected the results to be reciprocal and mutual. Just as they would benefit from the spiritual gifts he would bring and impart, so he would be encouraged by theirs. Paul desired a "brotherly exchange of spiritual gifts."[8] He knew that this exchange of charismata with new believers meant a new experience of grace and, hence, would be mutually strengthening. With this context in mind, Gotthold Hasenhüttl describes the charisma of 1:11 as "the charisma of encounter."[9] According to 1 Cor 12–14, Paul understood the primary purpose of charismata to be the upbuilding of the body. Thus, the double purpose "to be strengthened" and "to be mutually encouraged" belongs to the function of οἰκοδομή.

ROMANS 5:15, 16

The double usage of τὸ χάρισμα in these verses forms an essential element in the apostle's concern to contrast Adam and Christ. Contextually, vv 15 and 16 belong to Paul's central argument of dissimilarity between Adam and Christ.[10] In v 15 this dissimilarity is demonstrated between the trespass of the former (τὸ παράπτωμα) and the free gift of the latter (τὸ χάρισμα). Verse 16 further develops the contrast in terms of the effect: whereas the judgment of one man's sin led to condemnation, the charisma meant justification of the trespasses of all.

To understand adequately Paul's intent in using this term, one must refrain from isolating it from the liberal application of parallel expressions. No less than three nouns occur: δωρεά, δώρημα, and χάρις. Yet, opinions differ widely concerning the function and meaning of each.

One, if the first two are parallel in usage and meaning, the same is not true of χάρις. According to this interpretation, grace precedes the gift as event or disposition which makes possible and issues into giftedness.[11] The focus remains emphatically on grace as God's disposition from which he bestows the gift. And when Paul speaks of the gift bestowed, he uses δωρεά with the attributive clarification ἐν χάριτι, instead of χάρισμα as in the first antithetical statement of v 15. Likewise, δώρημα emerges as "gift" from χάρις and parallels χάρισμα in 16b. The latter serves as elucidation of the antithesis of 16a.[12] Χάρισμα, then, is functionally parallel with δωρεά and δώρημα.

The synonymity in meaning is not always accepted, however. English versions provide ample evidence of this fact. Often δωρεά and δώρημα are translated plainly as "gift," while χάρισμα is rendered as "free gift."[13] But such distinctions remain arbitrary and do not facilitate a better understanding of either term.[14] In fact, any distinction drawn between χάρισμα, δωρεά, and δώρημα does not affect the conclusion that in each case reference is made to the gift bestowed.

Two, Paul used charisma, as well as its parallels considered above, synonymously with χάρις. From this perspective, the former stands in hendiadic relation to χάρις τοῦ θεοῦ καὶ ἡ δωρεὰ ἐν χάριτι, and illustrates the verb περισσεύω. The emphasis lies in the superior power of grace, taking concrete shape in the gift. By the same token, the distinction between "grace" as disposition and "charisma" as gift bestowed is overcome. Following Käsemann, "charisma" in 15a should be "work of grace." In his translation of vv 15–16 the parallelism receives its full impact:

> The work of grace, of course, is not like the fall. For if through the fall of one many died, the grace of God, namely the gift granted with the gracious power of the one man Jesus Christ, abounded the more richly to many. What is given is not like that which the one sinner [did]. For judgement led from the one to condemnation, but the work of grace led from many transgressions to justification.[15]

While semantic synonymity may hardly be taken for granted, the apostle did use χάρισμα in thematic or contextual parallelism with χάρις. The terms are interchangeable in the context of vv 15–17, just as in Eph 4:7 Paul uses χάρις to express χάρισμα.

This leads to the third and most important aspect requiring attention. Neither the overlapping of χάρις and χάρισμα (or their nonparallelism) nor the synonymity of the various nouns used to express "gift" lessens the significance of the content of χάρισμα. In v 15 it is more difficult to pinpoint that content.

In keeping with the above discussion, it could be asserted that for Paul "charisma" contained everything embodied in "grace." But this line of argument proves fruitless. Another option, that of regarding "the one man Jesus Christ" as the gift which the apostle had in mind, does not arise directly from the context but seems to be projected on v 15 from 2 Cor 9:15.[16] While the idea cannot be dismissed altogether, the context of vv 16 and 17 requires a different emphasis. Rather than the person of Jesus Christ, what Paul has in view here is the gracious work of God in Jesus Christ in its most inclusive sense.[17] This gracious act of God takes on more specific character in v 16 where χάρισμα refers to the effect of God's act in those who respond to it, namely their acquittal[18] or their justification; i.e., the gift of righteousness (v 17).[19]

In the light of these observations, it is not sufficient to consider the noun χάρισμα strictly in terms of semantics. What provides the concept its broad sweep of meaning is Paul's ability to let it express contextually what he also described as "the grace of God" and that which received its concretion in the redemptive work of Jesus Christ.

ROMANS 6:23

At the conclusion of ch 6, Paul again uses χάρισμα as in 5:15, 16, in an antithetical statement. This time he draws the contrast[20] between the wages of sin,[21] in the form of death, and the gift of God, in the form of eternal life. The parallelism between 5:15, 16, and 6:23 is unmistakable, not only in the utilization of the antithesis in order to heighten the radically different character of χάρισμα from that of ὀψώνια, but even more in the comprehensive meaning that χάρισμα is given here.

In the statement "the gift of God is eternal life in Christ Jesus, our Lord," the apostle established the foundational charisma without which all or any other charismata cannot be received. Käsemann stresses this aspect without apology: "Other charismata only exist because of the existence of this one charism to which they are all related, and they only exist where the gift of eternal life is manifested in the eschatologically inaugurated dominion of Christ."[22]

Above all else, therefore, to have a charisma, for Paul, meant to partake of the life, grace, and Spirit of the risen Christ. In fact, the reception of true life coincides with the reception of the Holy Spirit. Both are charismatic in nature; neither of them can be separated from the grace of God.[23] No requirements are to be met for receiving the gift of eternal life. Thus what Rodman Williams notes concerning the gift character of the Holy Spirit applies conversely to Rom 6:23, "There are no conditions or requirements to be met, no stairs to climb or hoops to jump through, but simply the reception of a freely offered gift."[24]

Yet, to speak of eternal life as a charisma for the future without connotations for the present is as un-Pauline as it is to argue that the gift of acquittal or justification in 5:15, 16, means present enjoyment without implications for the future.[25] Precisely because Paul here used the term χάρισμα in the most comprehensive sense possible, he understood all gifts, present and future, to be received because of the grace of God under the one term. In other words, every provision of God is the believer's gift in Jesus Christ (Rom 8:32). Hence, on the basis of Rom 6:23, it is appropriate to describe as charismatic all who have received God's charisma of righteousness and, therefore, eternal life. The same broad perspective of charisma compelled the apostle to think of the Roman community of believers (and, therefore, of every Christian community he established) as no less than a charismatic community.[26]

ROMANS 11:29

Since Paul has demonstrated the capability of letting the expression "charisma" embrace God's gift to believers in its broadest sweep in 6:23, it comes as no surprise to find him applying it to Israel as a charismatic people. In so doing, he used the plural form for the first time in Romans.

It is clear that χαρίσματα here refers to certain manifestations of grace within Israel as the OT community of faith. And although nothing in the immediate context explains the need for the plural form (no listing of blessings or privileges is given), it is feasible that the apostle had in mind the gifts cited in 9:4: "Theirs is the adoption as sons; theirs the divine glory, the covenants, the receiving of the law, the temple worship and the promises."

With reference to the immediate context of v 28, both χαρίσματα and κλῆσις serve as further explanations of "election."[27] Brockhaus distinguishes between the two concepts as follows: "whereas χαρίσματα is the general description expressing the gift character of the differing gifts of the God of Israel to his people, κλῆσις is the special description expressing the theological value of the same gifts."[28] Considering Paul's entire argument on Israel's place in the context of the Christ event in chs 9–11, this distinction may be valid. At least this much affords certainty that 11:29, if not 11:28 and 11:29, constitutes the apostolic summary applicable to all three chapters. The specific meaning of χαρίσματα in this context, however, remains less certain. In general terms one may define it as the "acts of grace whereby God made Israel's calling and election sure."[29] Hence, for Paul these were irrevocable not only with reference to Israel's past but also with reference to Israel's future restoration. With the example of his own people's predicament, the apostle demonstrated the magnitude of God's grace manifested in Christ. Where Israel's disobedience abounded, the grace of God superabounded.[30] The charismata of God, then, are concrete manifestations of that grace experienced in Israel's past, and at the same time signals of their eschatological concretion.

ROMANS 12:6–8

Unfortunately this passage has often been subsumed under the general treatment of 1 Cor 12–14,[31] if not almost entirely ignored by interpreters of Romans.[32] But nothing in the context of Rom 12:6–8 suggests that the passage cannot stand on its own exegetical legs. It is striking, indeed, that Paul also dealt with a list of χαρίσματα here (although, for the most part, different from those in 1 Cor 12:8–10, 28–30, and Eph 4:11) within the context of the body analogy, as in 1 Cor 12:12–27.

Joachim Gnilka has raised the question of whether Paul had perhaps projected the Corinthian situation into that of Rome since the apostle wrote the Letter to the Romans from Corinth.[33] If the charge of such projection were true, however, Paul would have done so without knowing the conditions of the church in Rome as intimately as he did those in Corinth. Although it is significant that 12:3–8 belong to the opening of the paraenetic part of Romans, this does not permit the inference that the two church situations were analogous. Paul's style and argumentation in 1 Cor 12–14 are far more forceful than in Rom 12:6–8. The only possible hint of boastfulness about their use of χαρίσματα could be Paul's admonition, "Do not think of yourself more highly than you ought, but rather think of yourself with sober judgment, in accordance with the measure of faith God has given you" (12:3, NIV). But apostolic paraenesis does in no wise permit the a priori conclusion that there must have been trouble in Rome's community of believers. Rather, it may be reasonable to presume that Paul's elaborate discussion of χαρίσματα in 1 Corinthians was not merely tailor-made correction for the Corinthians but Paul's central concern for every church. The gifts' purpose could be none other than the upbuilding of the body by the members' fulfilling their enabling graces (χαρίσματα) toward each other, according to the grace given to them. Thus, while the Corinthian setting for the authorship of Romans may well be reflected in the 12:6–8 passage, there can be no doubt that this represents exhortation central to Paul's concept of charismatic giftedness.[34] This approach finds further support in Eph 4:11, 12, where the same concerns are evident.

The grammatical construction of the passage is awkward. Verse 6 opens with a participial clause (ἔχοντες δὲ χαρίσματα) and the paragraph ends without a single finite verb. One could take the opening participial clause coordinately with v 5, agreeing with ἔσμεν. In that case, a comma separates the two verses and the translation would be, "so we who are many are one body in Christ, and members of one another, having gifts. . . ." This possibility does not lend itself to smooth syntax, and makes for a more difficult translation of vv 7 and 8. Therefore, it is more appropriate to let the participle ἔχοντες introduce a new sentence which could begin with the participial phrase, "Having gifts" (RSV) or better, "Since we have gifts" (NASB). Either option necessitates the addition of hortatory imperatives for the remainder of the passage.[35] Each imperative would then correspond to the respective gift cited.

The list of seven gifts (prophecy, service, teaching, exhorting, encouraging, giving assistance or aid, showing mercy) describes the broad base of charismatic functions which Paul understood as part of the church's life and ministry. Only προφητεία occurs consistently in all of the lists. Surely this is not to say that Paul regarded the πνευματικά of 1 Cor 12:8–10 to be irrelevant or nonapplicable to the Roman Christians; rather, the χαρίσματα which he listed for the latter may have been particularly pertinent for their situation which the apostle may have understood with less specificity.

Before dealing with each gift briefly, two general observations require attention. One, προφητεία and διακονία are listed as nouns whereas the remaining five appear in the form of present participles. It may be argued that the nouns do not signify an individual charisma each, but perhaps two categories of gifts. Προφητεία would then be comprised of ὁ διδάσκων and ὁ παρακαλῶν, the latter term also expressing prophetic function in 1 Cor 14:3;[36] however, the correlation of ὁ διδάσκων with προφητεία cannot be substantiated explicitly.[37] In fact, the entire argument falters when a comparison with 1 Cor 12:28 is drawn. There, Paul first cited three gifts in terms of those fulfilling the functions of apostle, prophet, and teacher, and subsequently changed the pattern by citing five additional χαρίσματα by their nouns.

Paul's use of language in the lists of Rom 12:6–8 and 1 Cor 12:28 does not lend itself to an easy categorization of gifts, nor to the detection of patterns of distinction between gifts and the believer's charismatic functioning, if the comparison also includes Eph 4:11 where the gifts to the church appear to have been certain believers who carried out their functions (or charismatic offices?). Clearly, therefore, the apostle was able to describe χαρίσματα interchangeably by participial forms, by nominal designations, and/or by their bearers.

Two, Paul's overriding concern in this passage takes its cue from διάφορα, the adjectival modifier of χαρίσματα. Hence, the kaleidoscopic panorama of gifts in vv 6–8 fully justifies Paul's emphasis of the diversity of χαρίσματα in the church of Rome. The preceding body analogy in vv 4–5 constitutes the necessary prerequisite for χαρίσματα διάφορα.

For this reason it is premature to read into Romans an already developing or existing ministerial order.[38] There is no textual evidence whatsoever in 12:6–8 of a trend to institutionalize ministries, offices, or gifts. Such needless speculation is to be avoided. It is sufficient to affirm that Paul's paraenetic purpose was that bearers of different gifts were to function harmoniously for the upbuilding of the church.

Prophecy

Gerhard Friedrich considers prophecy the "most important charisma"[39] of the church. This is certainly no overstatement, considering the fact that Paul cited this gift consistently in his lists. Furthermore, Paul's detailed discussion of prophecy in 1 Cor 12–14 supports Friedrich's claim because of its communicability of God's message to the community of faith. It comes as no surprise that the apostle used it as his first example of the different gifts. Perhaps he had primarily this charisma in mind in Rom 1:11 since its intended purpose is the upbuilding, the encouragement, and the comforting of the body of Christ (1 Cor 14:3).[40]

If the meaning of prophecy is essentially subsumed under "preaching," Paul may have had a specific group of bearers in mind. From this supposition it is only a short step to regarding προφητεία as the function of the προφήτης; that is, a more or less established office in the church.[41] But there is no evidence in 12:6 that would lead one to regard prophecy as a fixed, institutional function. Even if the "prophetic office" is given status as "inaugural office" of the emerging church,[42] the separation of the prophets from the other charismatically endowed members of the church is arbitrary and thus not warranted.

Prophecy refers to the function of communicating revelations from

God[43] as a spontaneous utterance.[44] The factor of spontaneity seems to capture the idea of intelligible (and intelligent) communication under the inspiration of the Spirit (1 Cor 12:7, 11; 14:33),[45] as well as the proliferation of this charisma in the community—at least in Corinth (1 Cor 14:31, 39). The apostle provided prophecy with its "regulative principle";[46] it was to be used κατὰ τὴν ἀναλογίαν τῆς πίστεως.[47] Paul meant that when the prophet speaks God's word, he is not to go "beyond that which God has given him to speak."[48] The significance of discharging the prophetic function in "proportion to his faith" is summarized well by David Hill. He notes, "What Paul is saying then, is that the person who exercises the gift of prophecy should speak only when conscious of his words as inspired, and presumably only for as long as he is confident that God is speaking through him,"[49] thereby underscoring the factor of spontaneity.

The importance of prophecy for the early (and contemporary) Christian community can hardly be overestimated. Of all the gifts of inspired speech, none affects the spiritual well-being more than prophecy. Dunn feels so strongly about its centrality that he concludes, "Without it the community cannot exist as the body of Christ; it has been abandoned by God."[50] Other aspects of prophecy will be discussed under the exegesis of 1 Cor 12–14.

Service

Paul's mention of διακονία as one of the many different χαρίσματα is noteworthy insofar as it has quite a broad range of meaning and application in the Pauline correspondence itself. For instance, in 1 Cor 12:5 all gifts of the Spirit are described collectively as διακονία, thus establishing their fundamental purpose.[51] Yet it is only in his letter to the Romans that διακονία itself is said to be a χάρισμα, although Paul did not specify what he meant by διακονία. Did he understand it as a summary term for all ministries and for every act of ministry within the Christian community, so that every "work produced by faith" and "labor prompted by love" (1 Thes 1:3) of one member to another was, for Paul, an expression of this χάρισμα? Whether Paul was this inclusive or not cannot be determined. If he did have this universal meaning in mind, its designation as χάρισμα is questionable and unsuitable.[52]

It may also denote, although less likely here, the ministry of the Word, since Paul did, in fact, use the term with this meaning. He spoke of his own ministry as διακονία (Rom 11:13; 2 Cor 4:1; 5:18; Eph

4:12). The contextual setting of διακονία, following προφητεία and preceding διδάσκων, could be adduced in support.[53] But the basic meaning of διακονία moves in another, more practical, direction. It signifies "waiting at table" and therefore, more broadly, assistance or administration of help to physical needs.[54] Paul used it with this meaning freely when he referred to the financial assistance for the church in Jerusalem (Rom 15:25–31; 2 Cor 8:4; 9:1, 12, 13). In 1 Cor 16:15, the household of Stephanas is reported to have devoted itself to the διακονία τοῖς ἁγίοις, presumably by way of hospitality. Thus the basic meaning is "ministry to the needy" or "an act or acts of service in love." That this somewhat imprecise concept may have been foremost in Paul's mind in Rom 12:7 is further supported by the elaborate explanation of his ministry to the saints in Jerusalem which was the last major goal of his itinerary before setting sail for Rome (Rom 15:22ff).

Of course in the absence of a precise explanation of διακονία, one has to allow for the possibility that Paul could have had the practical, as well as the proclamational, aspects of διακονία in mind. Both are ministry or service, and both are directed to the believers as well as to Christ.[55]

A final observation must be noted regarding διακονία. The hortatory "let him serve" may have been Paul's way of admonishing believers in Rome to exercise this gift without jealousy for those whose gift was prominently carried out, publicly acknowledged, and respected. Διακονία is no less spiritual than προφητεία. The neglect of the former, because it does not receive the same attention as the latter, aborts the growth of the community. Prophetic ministry without practical ministry to the particular needs of the community misses the most basic criterion of ἀγάπη, in the Pauline churches as well as in the contemporary churches.

Teaching

Ὁ διδάσκων describes the function of expounding the Word of God; not as a new revelation from God, as in the case of prophetic ministry, but as the imparting of instruction based on truth already revealed. Recognizing the difficulty in separating some of these charismatic functions, C. K. Barrett links teaching with the succeeding charisma, namely ὁ παρακαλῶν. The former is the explanation of a truth; the latter is its application.[56] Similarly, Käsemann finds that the teacher cannot be distinguished from the prophet, and this in spite of 1 Cor

12:28 where the two are clearly separate.[57] Dunn compares prophecy and teaching as follows: "Prophecy would express a new word from God as such, whereas teaching would tend to denote more *a new insight into an old word from God*, into the traditions already accepted by the community as authoritative in some degree. . . ."[58]

Whatever the parameters of the teaching function may have been for Paul, he singled out ὁ διδάσκων to demonstrate the variety of χαρίσματα. And this fact ought to be sufficient for an acknowledgement that teaching is another form of dynamic, inspired communication of the message of the gospel of Jesus Christ. Whether teaching applied only to "charismatic exegesis"[59] of the OT, or to the entire treasure of Christian tradition[60]—including that of an oral nature, or both—can no longer be determined. It does not alter the fact that Paul considered teaching a concrete result of God's grace, however.

That Paul placed considerable importance on the gift of teaching becomes clearer when the list of χαρίσματα in Rom 12:6–8 is placed alongside those of 1 Cor 12:28–30, and of Eph 4:11 where teachers are mentioned again. If the apostles and prophets were the foundation of the church whose chief cornerstone was Jesus Christ, Paul may have conceived of teaching as the function responsible primarily for the building of the superstructure (Eph 2:20). Thus these young Christian communities would develop in the understanding of their faith through sound, dynamic instruction. They were established with apostolic and prophetic authority; now the same grace of God which enabled these ministries also provided for the continuity and growth of these communities. Therefore, exhorted Paul, those teaching were to give themselves fully to their charisma.[61]

Exhorting

What was established as one of the functions of προφητεία in 1 Cor 14:3 is here made a charisma all its own. Since prophecy and teaching are also cited, and ὁ παρακαλῶν follows the latter, Paul's understanding of this gift seems to have been fluid. How he carried out his function, if apart from teaching or prophecy, and how this gift became effective are not mentioned. The context may shed some light on the meaning of παρακαλέω. In 12:1 the apostle introduced the entire section of chs 12–15 with the emphatic statement παρακαλῶ οὖν ὑμᾶς, the position of the verb providing the emphasis. If παρακαλέω means "to exhort" or "to admonish" in 12:1, the same meaning may also be given in 12:8.[62] According to Otto Schmitz, παρακαλέω, with the meaning "to exhort," denotes both missionary proclamation and a certain "formula to introduce pastoral admonition."[63]

But Paul used this verb just as frequently with the meaning "to console," "to comfort," or "to encourage." This is clearly the tenor in 2 Cor 1:3–7 (perhaps the most sublime passage of comfort in the Bible) where Paul extolled God as the "God of all comfort who comforts us in all our affliction, so that we may be able to comfort those who are in any affliction, with the comfort with which we ourselves are comforted by God" (vv 3b, 4, RSV). The element of encouragement may also have been at the heart of what Paul meant by παράκλησις in 1 Cor 14:3.[64]

Rather than pitting one meaning against another, both "exhortation" and "encouragement" or "comfort" may be implied here, perhaps with an emphasis on the second meaning.[65] Consequently, in 12:8, ὁ παρακαλῶν may very well mean a "charisma of pastoral exhortation";[66] that is, one who exercises pastoral care, namely of the afflicted and distressed.[67]

Giving

The basic meaning of the verb μεταδίδωμι is "to give a part" or "to give a share of." The participle, then, means "one who gives of his own substance,"[68] and not so much the task of distributing community alms to the needy.[69] The attitude or disposition which was to govern such giving is ἐν ἁπλότητι. This term occurs in the NT only in Paul and only there in Romans, so that one may have to turn farther to ascertain the meaning of this qualifier. Its primary meaning is "with simplicity,"[70] "with singleness of purpose,"[71] or "wholeheartedly."[72] But in 2 Cor 8:2, 9:11–13, ἁπλότητι clearly requires the translation "liberality" or "generosity," and this may also be the meaning in Rom 12:8.[73] The latter meaning suits the subject ὁ μεταδιδούς better and may, in fact, be the determining factor in deciding which kind of giving Paul sought to designate as charisma.[74]

Leadership

Paul used ὁ προϊστάμενος as a further example of charismatic function within the community. But to what he may have referred is not entirely clear, as the English translations of the participle amply illustrate.[75] Basically and literally, πρόϊστημι means "to stand before." It is this basic meaning which emerges again in the resultant meanings "to rule," "to lead," "to direct," "to conduct," "to manage." Thus ὁ προϊστάμενος could denote "the one who leads" or, following the plural form in 1 Thes 5:12, "those over you in the Lord." "Leadership" is also the translation required in 1 Tim 3:4 where the reference is to elders who are to give exemplary leadership within their households or families as a qualification for office.[76] The χάρισμα Paul had in focus, according to this interpretation, was diligent (ἐν σπουδῇ) leadership in worship and in community affairs.

But an alternate meaning of προϊστάμενος, namely "the one who gives aid" (following the RSV), or "he who cares for others," may well be more appropriate in the context of 12:6–8.[77] It is surely not by chance that Paul inserted ὁ προϊστάμενος between ὁ μεταδιδούς and ὁ ἐλεῶν, both of which express the function of giving aid. The aspect of a father's caring for the other members of the family could be regarded as integral in 1 Tim 3:4. From this vantage point, Paul defined as χάρισμα the helpful caring for and aiding the "more defenseless members of the community (widows, orphans, slaves, strangers)."[78] Either way, he who exercises leadership, or he who cares for others, must do so ἐν σπουδῇ, with total dedication or abandon, with diligence, or with zest.[79]

Showing Mercy

Ὁ ἐλεῶν could refer to "acts of mercy" in general; or, since it is closely related to giving, the thought may be of a personal, direct ministry to the needy.[80] But such ministry is considered a χάρισμα only when carried out with cheerfulness (ἐν ἱλαρότητι).[81] Paul may have had Prov 22:8 ("God loves a cheerful giver") in mind, which he also quoted in 2 Cor 9:7. Practical expressions of mercy, for Paul, were not worked-up tokens of social concern for human plight but, rather, the concrete outworking of God's mercy freely bestowed and experienced. It is for this reason that Paul understood ὁ ἐλεῶν as an "enabling grace."

1 CORINTHIANS 1:7

Although Paul did not articulate what specific χαρίσματα he had in mind in 1:7, at least two of them seem to have been foremost in his thanksgiving for the Corinthians. In 1:5a he affirmed positively that the Corinthian community had been enriched in every way in Christ, and then elaborated more specifically in 1:5b, ἐν παντὶ λόγῳ[82] καὶ πάσῃ γνώσει. The affinity to 1 Cor 12:8–10 is unmistakable here, so that 1:7a represents a negative restatement of 1:5, namely "so that you lack in no gift." In this case, Paul did use χαρίσματα here as his preferred special or technical term;[83] that is, he used it as his summary term for the many gifts of grace for the upbuilding of the church. While it is possible to regard γνῶσις and λόγος as two "distinctive spiritual gifts or endowments,"[84] the apparent Corinthian preoccupation with speech-oriented expressions of spirituality requires ἐν παντὶ λόγῳ to be understood collectively of all inspired forms of utterance.

The sweeping assertion that the Corinthians lacked in no gift is no overstatement of the facts as Paul knew them from his own ministry in Corinth, for they had been given the grace of God in Christ Jesus. Thus, v 7 is the result of the establishment of the gospel in Corinth.[85] The apostle was not addressing a specific minority or faction; nor an individual within the community of faith in Corinth. Clearly, he addressed the church as a whole (the problem of divisions is not opened until 1:10) with the grateful acknowledgement that, as a community, they were not lacking any gift which the Spirit deemed necessary for their community. Probably Paul meant the diversity of gifts, or simply that there was no lack in the number of gifts.

The translation, "you *come short* in no gift of grace," which Barrett prefers, has some justification in the light of chs 12–14. He notes, "The troubles in Corinth were not due to a deficiency of gifts but to lack of proportion and balance in estimating and using them."[86] Nevertheless, in the context of Paul's εὐχαριστία for their fulness of experienced manifestations of God's grace, there is no need to read a tongue-in-cheek exaggeration into 1:7; and the general rendering of "not lacking in any spiritual gift" conveys the meaning adequately.

It is also significant that Paul leads from the affirmation of charismatic fulness directly into a participial clause concerning their eschatological hope and resultant life stance. They are said to lack in no χαρίσματα while eagerly awaiting the revelation of their Lord, Jesus Christ. Thus Paul placed the spiritual gifts in the context of the future —the eschaton—which, in turn, was to determine their attitude toward the use of special endowments for the present. Instead, the Corinthians were absorbed with the ecstasy and excitement of present experience at the expense of the future. Conzelmann noted correctly, "possession of χαρίσματα is not yet the realization of the eschaton but an earnest of what will be."[87] Paul had more to say on this relationship of grace gifts to the eschaton in ch 13. Thus, the possession or presence of charismata does not mean arrival at the apex of life in the Spirit but the work of the Spirit in the present, transforming the community as it eagerly awaits the Lord, engaged in active ministry (cf. 1 Cor 1:12).

1 CORINTHIANS 7:7

The mention of celibacy as a charisma immediately follows the expression of Paul's desire for all men to be like he was, namely, single. The discussion of celibacy and marriage, which began with 7:1, was precipitated by the Corinthians' letter to Paul. It may well be that a faction of the Corinthian Christians insisted on the uniformity of all believers in matters of sexual relations, teaching "It is good for a man not to marry" or more correctly, following the RSV, "not to touch a woman." Hence Paul's emphasis in 7:7b on the variety of gifts (each one has his own gift from God; one has this gift, another has that gift) was likely directly related to their claim.[88] Thus Paul defused the Corinthian tension by placing celibacy within the context of the grace of God and its concrete expressions.

But can celibacy per se be the charisma to which Paul was referring? Some interpreters have expressed a justified reluctance to jump to that conclusion. Not every celibate is necessarily supernaturally endowed; and it might be argued that celibacy, as well as marriage, is a matter of nature and not of charisma.[89] The generalization of celibacy here forces too much into the context. What Paul meant was the charisma of sexual continency "without which it was disastrous to remain unmarried."[90] When Paul commented, "One has this gift, another has that," he knew first of all that his own status was predicated upon a special grace gift from God. This particular charisma, therefore, uniquely fitted the calling upon him. In this context, MacGorman observes correctly, "It equipped him to fulfill his itinerant ministry as an apostle without undue distraction from sexual temptation."[91] Thus the purpose of sexual continency has as its foremost intention not the upbuilding of the body but the complete dedication to a ministry received. Οἰκοδομή, in this instance, becomes an indirect purpose.

The assertion continues to be made by many that when Paul described celibacy as a charisma with the phrase ὁ μὲν οὕτως, by implication the next phrase, ὁ δὲ οὕτως, rendered marriage also a charisma. They appeal to the context in which Paul made the statement to justify their claim.[92] From this assertion it is only a short step to including parenthood in the list of implied charismatic gifts.[93] In the broadest sweep possible, Jürgen Moltmann notes, "The Spirit makes the whole biological, cultural and religious life history of a person charismatically alive. . . ."[94] Yet, before such sweeping implications are approved, one needs to ask again if the exegesis of the text permits the practice. Paul's choice of expression (ὁ μὲν οὕτως, ὁ δὲ οὕτως) is too general to specify marriage as the only other logical possibility of charisma. Indeed, all that can be affirmed is that the reference is to "any special endowment for service other than that stated."[95]

The charisma of sexual continence receives its urgency from the eschatological background in which ch 7 is couched (e.g. v 26; vv 29–31). Consequently, in 1 Cor 7 Paul most probably did not even think of the upbuilding of the church as the purpose of celibacy. Rather, he saw as the primary purpose the utmost desire to please the Lord. Thus Hasenhüttl suggests, "the concern for the things of the Lord" does not mean work done in or for the church. Instead, to please the Lord means to live in a manner worthy of the Lord, "in order to belong fully to him."[96] While Hasenhüttl's interpretation should not be discounted, one can not but notice a subtle shift to a monastic conception of the gift of celibacy.[97]

In summary, Paul spoke of sexual continency (i.e. celibacy) as a charisma. Marriage is not, therefore, automatically also understood as grace endowment, at least not from 1 Cor 7:7. Paul probably had a much broader spectrum of gifts in mind. The purpose of celibacy as special enabling for service is commensurate with the special calling and ministry in the light of the eschatological condition. Paul held both ministry and lifestyle in focus. It is entirely foreign to Paul to divorce divine enabling for ministry from the same grace which enables worthy conduct.

1 CORINTHIANS 12–14

Although the concept of charismata, strictly speaking, is only found in ch 12, Paul wrote these chapters as a thematic unit;[98] they must be considered together. Nevertheless, primary attention will be given to ch 12, which undoubtedly constitutes the basis for the concerns of the two subsequent chapters.

Introducing the exegesis will be a brief look at the background of the Corinthian situation which may have occasioned Paul's longest and most thorough instruction on charismata. The interpretive considerations will treat the text as follows: (1) the christological test of spiritual giftedness

(12:1–3); (2) the fundamental character of gifts (12:4–6); (3) the lists of charismata (12:8–10, 28, 29–30); (4) the functional purpose of gifts (12:12–27); and (5) the realm of the gifts' operation (ch 13).

The Corinthian Situation

Probably one of the first questions asked by any serious student of 1 Corinthians pertains to the possible problem, or problems, in the Corinthian community of faith, which gave rise to Paul's correspondence.[99] A cursory reading of 1 Corinthians reveals problems of a church fragmented by divisions (1:10–4:21), by sexual immorality (5:1–13, 6:12–20), and by non-Christian judicial practice (6:1–11). These concerns were conveyed to Paul by "some from Chloe's household" (1:11). A letter from the Corinthian church reached Paul about the same time —likely through Stephanas, Fortunatus, and Achaicus (16:17)—seeking directives concerning matters of marriage and celibacy (7:1–40), of freedom to participate in heathen festivals by eating food sacrificed to idols (8:1–11:1), of misconduct in worship and celebration of communion (11:2–34), of flagrant denial of the resurrection (15:1–58), of the collection (16:1), and of Apollos' coming (16:12). Into this second list of concerns also belongs the flaunting of spirituality in the misuse of spiritual gifts (12:1–14:40). All but one of these areas Paul introduced with the formula περὶ δὲ τῶν.[100]

Some have sought to subsume all of the Corinthian problems under one particular theme. Walter Schmithals has offered the suggestion that gnosticism was the root problem in Corinth, which then expressed itself as noted above.[101] John MacArthur insists that all the problems of Corinth were cumulatively involved in Paul's discussion of πνευματικά. Hence, "the wilder and more agitated the person was, the more godly and spiritual he was supposed to be."[102] But such generalizations are hardly justified, let alone supported by the textual and historical evidence.

Other scholars have assessed the situation behind chs 12–14 more carefully by pointing out that the root problem was the abuse of glossolalia.[103] This χάρισμα was practiced by a group maintaining to be πνευματικοί, a sort of spiritual elite which was known by its inspired speech.[104] Generally, the inference is that these divisive pneumatics belonged to the educated social strata who may also have performed leadership functions within the Corinthian church.[105] However, recent sociological studies have shown very convincingly that the glossolalists were most likely not the educated but the illiterate converts, the slaves,

and the harbor workers who found in this gift a convenient and powerful means of expression in pneumatic worship.[106]

Walter J. Hollenweger has written a very creative narrative exegesis
based on sociological insights. He offers a reconstruction of the Corinthian church gatherings, the tensions and conflicts between the literate
and the illiterate groups of believers, and between the often uncontrolled
enthusiasm of the latter and the applicability of Paul's instructions read
by the former.[107]

Therefore, W. J. Bartling has perceived the Corinthian problem with
reference to chs 12–14 correctly as "a perverted vision of what charismatic endowment entails in congregational life. . . ."[108] It is in ch 12
that Paul set out to instruct the Corinthians regarding the function of
grace gifts within the community of faith.

The Christological Test of Spiritual Giftedness, 12:1–3

Two significant factors deserve attention with reference to this study:
One, the meaning of Paul's introductory τῶν πνευματικῶν (12:1), and
two, the supreme test for all claims to pneumatic endowment in the
confession Κύριος Ἰησοῦς (12:3).

(1) The Meaning of τῶν πνευματικῶν

At face value, without comparison with Paul's usage of the term
elsewhere in 1 Corinthians, the gender of the genitive of this adjectival
noun cannot be determined. Grammatically, it can be taken as a neuter
(spiritual things)[109] or as a masculine noun (spiritual men, persons).[110]
Barrett reflects an approach of "no decision," finding it impossible to
discover "objective ground for a decision between the two possibilities,
and little difference in sense is involved—spiritual persons are those
who have spiritual gifts."[111]

In 1 Corinthians, Paul used πνευματικός fifteen times in adjectival
or substantival form. As a masculine noun it occurs in 2:13–14 and
3:1, distinguishing spiritual persons from those who are not. In 14:37
Paul referred to those who are claiming to be prophets as πνευματικός.
Consequently, τῶν πνευματικῶν, in 12:1 could very well be a parallel
usage introducing the issue of the spiritual ones within the Corinthian
church who were gifted. If this is what Paul meant, the translation
should read, "And now concerning the pneumatics."[112]

But against this view militates the neuter usage of τὰ πνευματικά in
14:1 where Paul used the term clearly with reference to spiritual

matters—or, contextually more likely, to spiritual gifts. The neuter noun also occurs in 2:13, 9:11 (pl.), and 15:46 (sg.); yet, these references are not to charismatic endowment. It is quite possible that Paul considered πνευματικά and χαρίσματα as synonymous terms; all the more so since 12:31 uses the latter, and 14:1 the former, with the same basic thrust: "eagerly desire the (greater) gifts."

From the introductory formula and its subject matter, περὶ δὲ τῶν πνευματικῶν, it can also be argued that πνευματικά was the preferred term of the Corinthians, describing the character of their own experiences with the πνεῦμα. The term was also known outside of Paul in his lifetime, and belonged to the special vocabulary of incipient gnosticism.[113] Paul may have borrowed the term πνευματικά as a *terminus technicus* from Hellenism;[114] however, the apostle's use of the term in the Corinthian context hardly permits that option. Rather, it may be more correct to suppose that the spiritual elitists in Corinth, who were acquainted with πνευματικά as technical term from their pre-Christian experiences, imposed their category on the community's understanding of charismata. Paul, therefore, used their category to meet them on their own turf, as it were.

If Paul intended their favored term to serve as a paraenetic bridge, the translation of 12:1 could read, "Now about what you call the 'spiritual gifts.' . . ."[115] In still sharper contrast, John Ruef speculates that the Corinthians asked Paul about spiritual men and Paul instructed them about gifts.[116] If the argumentation is valid that Paul introduced the subject of spiritual endowment by the Corinthian technical term πνευματικά, the shift to χαρίσματα in 12:4 may indeed denote his preference for the term which he considered more appropriate to describe giftedness.[117]

It must be pointed out that Paul did not discard the Corinthian term, however; gifts which the Holy Spirit bestowed were none other than the enabling graces of which Paul spoke elsewhere. The functional parallelism between πνευματικά and χαρίσματα must, therefore, be maintained. But in 12:2 Paul provided a glimpse into the possible cause for his preference of the term χαρίσματα, since πνευματικά may have been the general term describing religious, especially ecstatic, experience in paganism. Yet, instead of discarding "spiritual gifts," Paul instructed the Corinthians on the correct perspective and position of πνευματικά with reference to Jesus Christ.

(2) The Christological Test

The genuine "speaking by the Spirit of God" confessed and exalted the Lord Jesus Christ. Phenomena of the pneumatic realm, primarily evidenced in ecstatic speech, also belonged to the Corinthians' past, pagan experience. Thus Paul placed such manifestations in their totality —not only those of the realm of speech—under the test of christological confession. Speaking by the Spirit of God without confessing Κύριος Ἰησοῦς is a contradiction in terms. The one is impossible without the other. Traugott Holtz regards this as the most common sign of where the Spirit is at work. "Where Jesus is rejected, the Spirit cannot be at work."[118]

But what does one make of the negative confession; that is, of the curse Ἀνάθεμα Ἰησοῦς? Did Paul merely employ it as an "antithetical construction of analogy" to highlight the confession Κύριος Ἰησοῦς?[119] In that case, the curse formula would amount to little more than a "hypothetical opposite,"[120] employed "only for the sake of argument."[121] However, it is difficult to believe that Paul would choose such a drastic statement for the purpose of rhetorical contrast alone.

That Paul made the statement is sufficient indication, maintains P. E.-B. Allo, that the curse was actual and referred to the Christian ecstatics who were resisting the oncoming ecstasy. He finds a convenient example in Sybil "who foamed as she resisted the inspiration that was taking possession of her. . . ."[122] The problem with this argument, however, is that it injects more into the text than the context allows. Paul seemed to draw a clear line of distinction between former pagan experience in v 2 and the Christian, pneumatic experience in v 3. All attempts at explaining away the negative curse as hypothetical, and of charging that certain Corinthian pneumatics cursed Jesus in their ecstasy, remain speculative.

From the syntactical construction of v 3, the following observations are noteworthy. In 3a Paul expressed something about those who spoke pneumatically—that is, in or by the Spirit—namely, that they could not say Ἀνάθεμα Ἰησοῦς. In 3b the stress is on those who confess Κύριος Ἰησοῦς, and Paul declared that such confession is uttered in or by the Holy Spirit. Along these lines Brockhaus interprets Paul as saying in v 3, "You do not need to fear, I can assure you, that a pneumatic gives himself to cursing in his ecstasy. Rather, all of you who confess Jesus as the Lord, are under the active influence and clear leading of the Holy Spirit."[123] Thus, the prominence of 12:1–3 established Paul's basis for the rest of ch 12. Perhaps not least in Paul's mind was the intent to put at ease those Corinthians who were concerned about their fellow Christians endowed by the Spirit with gifts of inspired speech.

The Fundamental Character of Gifts, 12:4–6

What Paul called πνευματικά in 12:1 he named χαρίσματα in v 4. Already he has established that the primary test of the gifts of the Spirit is the confession of Jesus as Lord.[124] It does not seem adequate to consider the two terms as an example of Pauline parallelism without further explanation. Rather, having subsumed the πνευματικά to the Lordship of Christ, he proceeded, in v 4, to χάρις. All boasting for self-effort and self-desert are eliminated, for endowment for service is as much by grace as are salvation and growth.[125]

Utilizing three parallel sentences in which the term for "gift" and that for "giver" change each time, Paul sought to express the character of charismata as "manifoldly different operations and manifestations."[126] While the parallelism among χαρίσματα, διακονίαι, and ἐνεργήματα is unmistakable, there is little justification for Lietzmann's assertion that "only rhetorical requirements have caused the differentiation of pneumatic manifestations."[127] Conzelmann has more appropriately suggested that it is the content which determined Paul's usage of these parallel concepts.[128]

Χαρίσματα, Paul's preferred concept for describing giftedness, conveyed his idea of grace-relatedness here as much as in previous usage. The context may well allow for regarding the term here as more specific or technical than where no lists of gifts are in focus.[129]

Διακονιῶν denotes the fundamental purpose for God's gracious bestowal of gifts. Only in different kinds of service exists the legitimization of charismata. Heinz Schürmann has observed that, for Paul, "there can be no 'kinds of service' which are not charisms wrought by the Spirit";[130] and Oudersluys noted that "a person's gift becomes his ministry."[131]

Ἐνεργημάτων describes the concrete effects which occur when χαρίσματα are used in service. Hence the translation "apportionments of activities"[132] is misleading because it seems to approve of all activity in church as charismatic. But what Paul probably sought to establish was the fact that God energizes all enabling graces; thus, charismata become demonstrations of the power of God,[133] effected in service.

The giver of spiritual gifts, according to Paul, is the one Spirit, the one

Lord, and the one God who works all things in all people. The trinitarian (likely unintentional) ascription to the Godhead of giving gifts for service is striking, but it may not represent Paul's primary intent in the passage. It is more probable that the emphatically placed αὐτό—αὐτός —αὐτός carried the weight of Paul's intended meaning and thus presaged the body analogy in vv 12–27. Differing gifts energized by God, for different kinds of service, find their unifying center in "the Spirit who gives, the Lord who is served, the God who is at work. . . ."[134]

The Lists of Χαρίσματα, 12:8–10, 28, 29–30

As many as six lists of gifts have been established in chs 12–14. But for the sake of brevity and to avoid unnecessary repetition, the enumeration of certain gifts in 13:1–3, 14:6, 26, will not be included in this study since most of them are also cited in 1 Cor 12 or Rom 12:6–8. This leaves three related lists to be considered; namely 1 Cor 12:8–10, 12:28, and 12:29–30. Since the concept of charisma appears in each list, specifically with reference to "gifts of healing," the procedure will follow the same order as in Rom 12:6–8; each gift will be dealt with briefly.

(1) 1 Corinthians 12:8–10

Paul cited nine gifts in this, his longest, list of grace endowments. Traditional Pentecostal exegesis still tends to set these apart from the rest of the gifts mentioned by Paul. Accordingly, following Paul's introduction of the topic in 12:1, they maintain that these nine gifts are uniquely the "spiritual gifts," or the "gifts of the Spirit"; whereas the other gifts are characterized as "ministry gifts," "charismatic gifts," or "motivational gifts."[135] The Pauline link of charismata with πνεῦμα in 12:4 invalidates such arbitrary distinctions. Verse 7, as transition from 12:4–6 to 12:8–10, also negates such differentiation. The manifestation of the Spirit, namely in differing kinds of charismata, is given to every one for the common good. Thereby Paul effectively eliminated every form of structuring these gifts into a hierarchy of values.[136]

(a) *Utterance of wisdom.* Wisdom per se was one of the watchwords of the Corinthians; this is at least a reasonable inference to be drawn from Paul's treatment of "wisdom" in 1 Corinthians.[137] But it must be noted that it is not σοφία which is sanctioned in 12:8a;[138] rather, the utterance or the word of wisdom is in focus. Thus the charisma consists not in wisdom as the content of the utterance but in the actual utterance of wisdom which becomes a shared experience because it results in the upbuilding of the body.[139]

What, then, was the content of the λόγος σοφίας as Paul's reaction to the Corinthian σοφία? From 1 Cor 1-3 it is almost certain that Paul identified the wisdom from God with God's saving deed in the crucified Christ, particularly in the proclamation of the saving event (e.g. 1 Cor 1:18-25). While Paul did not elaborate on what he meant by "the utterance of wisdom" in 12:8, it is reasonable to infer that he did have in mind the inspired communication of God's redemptive decrees,[140] especially that of the cross.

(b) *Utterance of knowledge.* Like σοφία, γνῶσις belonged to the slogans of the Corinthians, perhaps of one of the factions opposing Paul, as described in 1:12. The Corinthian emphasis of knowledge can be inferred with relative certainty from 1 Cor 8:1ff and 13:2, 8; hence, γνῶσις was "charismatic insight into the real nature of reality, into the structure of the cosmos and the relationship of divine and human, spiritual and material within that cosmos."[141] Banks interprets the λόγος γνώσεως in terms of "understanding the Old Testament, Christian traditions and the capacity to expound them correctly."[142] But according to the usage of the noun γνῶσις in 1 Corinthians, Banks' suggestion hardly reflects Paul's intent.

Schürmann views γνῶσις in 12:8 as "pneumatic understanding, from the depth of the human spirit, directed more toward the practical."[143] It is quite obvious that the distinctions between the λόγος σοφίας and the λόγος γνώσεως begin to fade at this juncture; for to declare the one more practically oriented than the other is to exceed the contextual boundaries.

Some interpreters, consequently, have argued that there exists no distinction between the two utterances since it is impossible to say whether and how Paul distinguished between them.[144] The use of two different prepositions (διά and κατά) for the respective utterances provides no warrant for distinctions between σοφία and γνῶσις. Both prepositional phrases, διὰ τοῦ πνεύματος and κατὰ αὐτὸ πνεῦμα, express the agency of the Spirit by which God gave these charismata. Whatever the particular nature of the γνῶσις may have been, it was the inspired utterance of knowledge for the common good which Paul considered a gift of the Spirit.

(c) *Faith*. When Paul named πίστις a spiritual gift, he did not refer to saving faith but perhaps to the faith which can move mountains (1 Cor 13:2). Hence the faith referred to in 12:9 could be described as "charismatic faith,"[145] provided it does not imply a relegation of justifying faith to a lesser degree of spirituality. On the other hand, the generality of faith as the believer's relationship to God, although miraculous, does not automatically guarantee that every believer is charismatically endowed with πίστις. The introductory pronoun ἑτέρῳ requires a differentiation.

It would seem that πίστις as charisma does not function independently. Its placement is noteworthy in this connection; it precedes the gifts of healing and the miracles or mighty works. Charismatic faith may, therefore, denote a "mysterious surge of confidence"[146] that God will grant a healing or a miracle. But if Paul connected faith with expressions of divine action on behalf of the community, he must have held the same view on faith's relationship to the various forms of inspired speech.[147] Faith as a gift of the Spirit seems to be an attendant charisma. Conzelmann has perceived that correctly in noting that "faith is a gift alongside others."[148]

(d) *Gifts of healing*. It is significant that Paul did not state this gift simply with the descriptive designation ἰαμάτων, or perhaps ἐνεργήματα ἰαμάτων. This is the only gift carrying the characteristically Pauline term χαρίσματα, perhaps to avoid the tendency to regard healing as an end in itself. That this particular expression of "giftedness" occurs in vv 9, 28, and 30 may point to the importance which either the Corinthians or Paul, or both, attributed to it.

The plural χαρίσματα ἰαμάτων is significant for at least two considerations. One, the indefinite plural denies the notion of elevation to the status of a singular healer for all illnesses; the gifts of healing are sovereignly bestowed upon some believers commensurate with the illnesses present, either in number or kind. Two, these gifts are meant for service for the good of the community. Therefore, this endowment was not designed to be a demonstration of power per se, but, as Hasenhüttl notes, "authoritative ministry directed to others,"[149] in the same venue that messianic healings were God's gracious healing activity through Jesus for those in need of healing.[150]

(e) *Miracles*. The Greek ἐνεργήματα δυνάμεων suggests a more precise translation, "miraculous works," or "mighty works." The fact

that Paul listed them separate from the "gifts of healing" indicates that
they did not connote the same. While the latter may be more concerned
with the realm of human existence in its totality, the former seems to
refer rather to the powerful displays of God's δύναμις in humanity's
environment. The reference may be to the "overcoming of the power of
the evil one through the saving power of God";[151] that is, the gracious
manifestation of God's power of exorcism.

But humanity's environment included both the spiritual (demonic)
and the natural realm. The gift of miracles certainly included the "nature
miracles."[152] In Rom 15:9 Paul attested to the occurrence of "mighty
works" in his own ministry.

Most important of all, the apostle incorporated this gift constructively
into his catalogue of gifts designed to strengthen the community of
faith. Paul never intended it to become the *raison d'être* of professional
miracle workers and healing artists.

(f) *Prophecy*. The basic thrust of προφητεία has already been dealt
with in the context of Rom 12:6. That Paul mentioned "prophecy" or
its bearers, the prophets, three times in 1 Cor 12 points to the importance he must have accorded this gift. In addition, much of ch 14 is
devoted to the insistence of Paul that prophecy must be considered the
preferred form of communication in the context of the corporate gathering of the church. Preference is accorded because prophecy is intelligible whereas glossolalia is unintelligible, although both are forms of
inspired speech because both are given by the Spirit.

It is significant to observe that the listing of prophecy here does not
yet reflect the priority which elevated it in ch 14. In keeping with the
earlier comment that Paul listed the gifts in vv 8–10 at random, with
the sole purpose of stressing the diversity of gifts given by the one
Spirit, the meaning of "prophecy" (and its placement between "miracles"
and "discernment of spirits") does not exceed that of προφητεία in
Rom 12:6.

The argument that "prophecy" enjoys a higher status in 12:10 since
it denotes the activity of the prophets whom Paul ranked second only to
the apostles in 12:28, and who clearly represented an established order
within the early church, has little to commend itself.[153] Otherwise it
would be difficult to understand Paul's desire, expressed to the entire
church in 14:5, "I would like every one of you to speak in tongues but I
would rather have you prophesy," and his concessive advice in 14:31,

"For you can all prophesy in turn so that everyone may be instructed and encouraged."

On the other hand, of course, Paul made it very clear in 12:29 that not all were prophets, because such an assumption would make a mockery of the need for, and of the divine provision of, a diversity of gifts. At least this much can be established from chs 12–14: Paul did not distinguish rigidly between the gift of prophetic utterance and the prophets —either as bearers of the gift of prophecy in the community at large or as those who held a recognized office.

The preeminence of the prophets in Corinth is asserted by E. Earle Ellis on the basis that the πνευματικοί of 12:1 were identical to the prophets. Together with those who taught or spoke in tongues, or interpreted tongues, the prophets were persons empowered to speak τῷ πνεύματι. Thus Ellis finds it significant that those whom Paul placed first in the church—namely apostles, prophets, and teachers (12:28) —are characterized by pneumatic gifts.[154] But Ellis' suggested parallelism seems forced and superimposed upon the text, since all charismata are given by the Holy Spirit, and it is not permissible, therefore, to single out a few gifts (e.g., of inspired utterance) and to declare them pneumatic.

In an incisive form-critical study, Ulrich B. Müller has endeavored to establish that NT prophecy in general and Pauline prophecy in particular are analogous to the function of proclamation. He defines prophecy as hortatory proclamation in the community and as proclamation of judgment and salvation.[155] Müller's thesis is essentially based on three factors: one, on his translation of προφητεύω as "to proclaim prophetically" (e.g. 1 Cor 14:1, 3); two, on the effects of such activity in the church, namely its upbuilding, exhortation, and consolation (1 Cor 14:3); and three, on the essence of prophetic proclamation, namely the conviction of sinners and their confession, "God is truly among you" (14:24, 25). While the basic tenor of Müller's treatment is noteworthy, it lacks recognition of the element of spontaneity which characterizes the activity of the Spirit. Prophecy, for Paul, meant not so much a prepared sermon, as a word of revelation from God for a specific occasion or situation and spontaneously uttered for the upbuilding of the body.[156]

Some scholars understand the Pauline prophetic function in terms of the authoritative OT prophets, stressing the continuity between the OT prophetic message and that of the NT.[157] The paraenetic character of prophecy as παράκλησις certainly has its precedent in OT prophecy. But it appears that the argument for continuity has to be stretched considerably when the gift of prophetic utterance, as Paul understood it, is in view. The authority which the OT prophet claimed in his message, introduced and indicated by the formula, "thus says the Lord," is nowhere accorded to the Corinthian prophets; nor to any others. Indeed, Paul instructed clearly in 14:29 that prophetic utterance was subject to spiritual evaluation of the message and of the source of its inspiration.[158]

Gerhard Dautzenberg has proposed an entirely different understanding of prophecy. Maintaining that "the structure of prophetic understanding in 1 Cor 12–14 is closely related to the scope of apocalyptic knowledge arising from the Qumran writings, Philo, Josephus and the apocalyptic writings," he asserts that prophecy was tantamount to the utterance of mysteries (1 Cor 13:12) and of enigmatic riddles.[159] In order to communicate these to the community in an intelligible manner, the accompanying gift of διάκρισις πνευμάτων was essential. He gave the latter a corresponding new meaning, too; discernment of spirits became to prophecy what interpretation was to tongues. In other words, the prophetic gift of understanding mysteries and riddles cannot function on its own; it must be augmented by the gift of interpreting revelations or mysteries.

Dautzenberg supports his novel approach almost exclusively by examples from the field of the history of religions, and he has great difficulty in maneuvering the context of 1 Cor 12–14 to match his claims. Nowhere did Paul even intimate that prophecy was in need of a supportive charisma like tongues was. In fact, the apostle drew the contrast not between prophecy (as the lesser gift) and discernment (as the greater gift), but between prophecy as intelligible, inspired utterance and tongues as unintelligible, inspired utterance. Paul regarded prophecy, not discernment of spirits, as fully adequate to edify the church without the aid of a supplemental gift.[160]

The significance of prophecy as "gift of the Spirit" emerges from 1 Cor 14, Paul's longest and most detailed treatment of the matter. The salient points may be summarized as follows:

One, prophecy has priority over tongues because it communicates clearly God's Word (revelation) to the church directly, without the aid of other gifts to clarify what has been said (14:1–6).

Two, the purpose of prophecy is threefold: (1) It builds up the community of faith as a whole; (2) it includes the noninitiate (nonglossolalist) believer in the upbuilding; (3) it communicates effectively the claims of the gospel of Christ to the unbelievers who will be convicted and who will ultimately worship God (14:3–25).

Three, prophecy is as much subject to orderliness in the gatherings of the corporate body as is tongues because the prophet is rationally in control of what he utters and because he submits to the Lord, recognizing his own limitations (14:26–33, 37–40).[161]

(g) Discernment of spirits.

James D. G. Dunn translates διάκρισεις πνευμάτων as "evaluation of inspired utterances," and links it closely to the preceding utterance of prophecy.[162] Διάκρισις may indeed be correlated with prophecy; in 1 Thes 5:20, 21, Paul mentioned the necessity of testing or evaluating all things, which follows immediately after the exhortation, "Do not treat prophecies with contempt." There may be precedent, therefore, for the restrictive interpretation suggested by Dunn.

But against such a narrow conception speaks the fact that Paul did not elaborate on precisely what he meant by this gift in 12:10.[163] The need for Spirit-led evaluation of all χαρίσματα is held in abeyance. Dunn's view does not answer how the counterfeits or the genuine gifts other than prophecy would be detected for what they were. The ability to test whether the gifts manifested were from God, from a demonic source, or merely reflecting a human opinion was surely important not only for prophetic utterance but for all gifts.

Dautzenberg's notion was mentioned previously. His equally restrictive conclusion that διακρίσεις πνευμάτων means "charismatic interpretation of revelations given by the Spirit"[164] is unacceptable since it cannot be substantiated from the context of 1 Cor 12–14; nor from the entire Pauline corpus. Philonic references to the use of διακρίνω in terms of ability to interpret revelations and dreams constitute insufficient evidence for superimposing the same on Pauline usage of the above verb.

In the light of the test which Paul had already established in 12:3, it is more appropriate to stay with the meaning given by most interpreters. Accordingly, discernment of spirits means the Spirit-given ability to distinguish the Spirit of God from a demonic spirit, under whose direction the charismatic exercises a particular gift.[165]

Dunn proposes three practical criteria of evaluation (which may have been the Pauline measuring stick) to show how this charisma possibly operated. What Dunn applies to inspired utterance only, however, this writer suggests be expanded to all gifts:

1. Test of kerygmatic tradition: Does it exalt Jesus? (1 Cor 12:3)
2. Test of character: Does it manifest love? (1 Cor 13:4–7)
3. Test of οἰκοδομή: Does it build up? (1 Cor 14)[166]

(h) *Different kinds of tongues.* From the instructions Paul gave in chs 12–14 concerning γένη γλωσσῶν, the conclusion can hardly be contradicted that "speaking in tongues" was a major problem in the Corinthian practice of worship.[167] Evidently the glossolalist faction — perhaps identified as those who claimed to follow Christ in an elitist fashion (1:12) — regarded "tongues" as the communication with God *par excellence*, perhaps precisely because no one understood what they spoke. Glossolalia became conspicuous because of the glaring absence of love and because it was practiced with proud self-glorification while depreciating others. Thus, the unity of the body was woefully ignored; internal confusion among the members and external ridicule by outsiders were the inevitable results. Glossolalia was elevated as the supreme manifestation of the Spirit, at the expense of charismatic diversity (12:4). Such abuse of God's endowment of grace, Paul seemed to say in 12:3, is no longer demonstrative of the acknowledgment, "Jesus is Lord."

What did Paul believe glossolalia was? His interpreters differ widely in their answers to this question. Some have proposed that, true to the basic meaning of the term γλῶσσα, Paul thought of tongues as "speaking in other languages,"[168] either human[169] or angelic.[170] Perhaps γένη (different kinds) means a variety of either or both.

Others have concluded that Paul must have conceived of γλῶσσα as "the broken speech in religious ecstasy," which was, therefore, unintelligible.[171] The apostle's counsel in ch 14, as well as Paul's allusion in 12:2 to the Corinthians' former pagan practices, would support this view.

Still others identify tongues with prayer.[172] While ecstasy may have played a large part in the Corinthian usage of tongues, Paul's teaching bears out that ecstatic symptoms were not always a necessary ingredient. For instance, Paul asserted that "the spirits of the prophets are subject to the control of the prophets" (14:32), a criterion equally applicable to the glossolalic utterance. Hollenweger has emphasized this point, noting that "there exists not only a 'hot' speaking in tongues (which can be described as ecstatic although the person speaking in tongues is never 'outside himself'), but also 'cool' speaking in tongues, sometimes mystical, and sometimes sounding like an incomprehensible foreign language."[173]

It is noteworthy that Paul did not overreact to the Corinthian abuse of glossolalia by eradicating it altogether. Recognizing its value as one of the many enabling graces of God, he sought to correct and rechannel the gift for its orderly incorporation into their gatherings (14:26). He thanked God that he spoke more in tongues than they (14:18) and wished that they all spoke in tongues (14:5). Paul also affirmed that the one speaking in tongues speaks to God, thus edifying himself (14:2, 4). But this was not the foremost concern of the apostle. In ch 14 he demonstrated unequivocally that the οἰκοδομή of the community must be the regulative principle for the gift of tongues (14:5–12, 16, 17, 19). It may have been for the purpose of correcting the Corinthian imbalance caused by an overemphasis of tongues that Paul placed this gift last (together with its attendant gift, the interpretation of tongues) in the catalogues of 12:8–10 and 12:29–30. Another possible reason may be that tongues represents the only charisma which is not capable of upbuilding the church on its own. In order to fulfill its purpose in the corporate setting, it must be accompanied by the gift of interpretation to make clear what the glossolalist has uttered.

(i) *Interpretation of tongues.* As a gift of the Spirit, ἑρμηνεία γλωσσῶν functions only in a supplementary, but necessary, role. In this sense it is, like tongues, restricted in usage. Yet, what makes interpretation of tongues indispensable is its function of communicating intelligibly and intelligently, with the mind, what was uttered in the Spirit, by the glossolalist. It is the interpretation of tongues which edifies; therefore, at least in terms of effect, it becomes a gift equivalent to prophecy.[174] Nevertheless, the essential directional difference between prophecy and interpretation of tongues must be maintained. The former is God's revelation addressed to persons in their need, whereas the latter is the intelligible communication of glossolalic utterance addressed to God.

The basic meaning of the noun ἑρμηνεία is not so much "translation," as in the case of a foreign language, but "interpretation" or "explanation." Likewise, διερμηνευτής (14:28) does not correspond to "translator."[175] Based on his studies of Philo and Josephus, Anthony Thiselton has advanced the alternate meaning of 'to put into words' for ἑρμηνεία.[176] But there may not be as much new ground broken as Thiselton proposes, for "to put into words" and "to explain" are but different expressions of the same notion.

(2) 1 Cor 12:28

Immediately following the lengthy analogy of the body (vv 12–27) and as logical application of the principles involved, Paul proceeded to list another series of enabling graces. Of the eight examples, five —namely prophets, teachers, mighty works, gifts of healing, and tongues —have already been dealt with. Only the three remaining charismata —namely apostles, helps, and administration—will be considered below.

(a) *Apostles*. Both here and in Eph 4:11, apostles are mentioned first. The emphatic use of πρῶτον in 12:28 strongly suggests that Paul accorded the apostolic function a very special place. In 1:1 he established that his apostleship was predicated upon God's special call and commission. He outlined his ministry as an apostle in 3:10 as follows: "By the grace God has given me I laid a foundation as an expert builder." Yet, Paul never described his apostleship as a charisma. On the other hand, there is no evidence either that he excluded his apostleship from the charismatic framework of ministry.

It is not likely that Paul had in mind the circle of twelve apostles to whose number he considered himself added by God (1 Cor 15:7–9). Rather, congruent with the meaning of ἀπόστολος, derived from the verb ἀποστέλλω ("to send forth"), namely "one who is sent forth," Paul meant that those sent forth to preach the message of the cross were fulfilling a charismatic function.[177] However, there is no need to distinguish sharply between the restricted and the broader meaning of the term since Paul was not explicit. Yet if, with the prepositional phrase ἐν τῇ ἐκκλησίᾳ, Paul did not mean the church of Corinth per se, but the universal church, the second, broader concept of ἀπόστολος would seem more appropriate.[178] The context of ch 12 further supports this conclusion.

One additional point is worth noting. The specific enumeration of apostles, prophets, and teachers has often been taken in support of established offices.[179] However, nothing in the context bears out this assumption. James Moffatt notes that "when Orientals enumerated several things or persons, they often spoke of the first three especially (e.g., Gen 32:19, Mt 22:25)."[180] Again, Paul provided no clear lines of demarcation; the intended stress was on the charismatic function of an apostle, rather than on the apostle's preeminence.

(b) *Those able to help others*. The term ἀντιλήμψεις occurs only here in the NT, and may be best translated as "helpful deeds." The emphasis seems to be on the acts or deeds, rather than on persons.[181] Perhaps Paul had in mind the same type of charismatically endowed function as the last three mentioned in Rom 12:6–8. If this assumption is correct, the gift of helpful deeds was directed toward the needy in the community of faith.[182]

(c) *Those with gifts of administration.* Again, κυβερνήσεις, like the preceding term, is found only here in the NT. Its occurrence seems to be equally sparse in secular Greek usage. The translation "administration" takes its cue from the Greek κυβερνήτης, meaning "steersman" or "helmsman" (e.g., Acts 27:11; Rev 18:17).[183] Therefore, this particular charisma entailed the function of giving direction or leadership, and may be akin to προϊστάμενος in Rom 12:8.

The last two functions may, following Barrett's suggestion, foreshadow the later work of deacons and elders.[184] But the context of 1 Cor 12 itself does not contain any such allusions, so that it seems best not to bias the evidence with exegetical speculation.

(3) 1 Cor 12:29–31

Two points deserve a closer look in this third list of charismata, all of which Paul mentioned previously. One, the use of the negative particle μή with each of the seven gifts listed renders each a rhetorical question. The English versions render these as straightforward interrogatives (e.g., "Are all apostles?"), but thereby they sacrifice the clarity of Paul's actual intent. A literal translation capturing the rhetorical impact would read, "Not all are apostles, are they?" the expected but omitted answer being, "Of course not." Thus the apostle brought the subject of charismatic endowment back to his central concern; gifts are given by God through his Spirit to each one, as he desires. Hence, "there are no every-member gifts."[185]

Two, based on this fact, Paul admonished the Corinthians to desire earnestly τὰ χαρίσματα τὰ μείζονα. Which gifts he meant cannot be determined with certainty. But if the purpose of gifts is to correspond to the analogy of the body (vv 12–27), the "greater gifts" probably referred to those endowments which built up the church in an intelligible and intelligent manner.

The Functional Purpose of Gifts, 12:12–27

Through the analogy of the human body, Paul endeavored to illustrate how charismata were to function in the context of the community of believers in Corinth. Admittedly, the term itself is never mentioned in vv 12–27; but no one will seriously question that Paul's concern was indeed functional, not polemical. In 12:4–11 the apostle emphasized that all gifts, however diverse they might be, were bestowed by the Holy Spirit for one purpose; namely their functioning for the common good. Further, in vv 28–30 the logical conclusions which are applied arise from the principles exemplified in the preceding passage.[186]

In order for Corinthians to understand the analogy, Paul had to establish first that their initiation into the body of Christ came about sovereignly and miraculously by the Holy Spirit (v 13). The unity of the one body received its greatest asset in the diversity of those who constituted that body.

Verses 14–27 seem to convey two principles crucial to the harmonious functioning of the body. One, there is no room for inferiority complexes (vv 14–20).[187] Nonidentical functions of individual members, compared with those of others, do not necessitate, much less permit, nonfunction. Just as it is absurd to think that a few prominent limbs make up the whole body, so it is absurd to think that the body of Christ can function when certain gifts are neglected because they appear to be less prominent than others. Paul crowned his argument with the emphatic statement that "God has arranged the parts of the body, every one of them, just as he wanted them to be" (v 18). Refusal to use the grace endowment(s) which God has given to the individual, for any reason, means to ignore God's greater concern for the whole. Brockhaus' interpretive paraphrase of Paul's intent captures Paul's concern aptly:

> Those of you with functions that receive less attention, do not underestimate your significance! Stop thinking that you are superfluous because of the respected church functions. Your functions are not, therefore, less important for the existence of the community.[188]

Two, there is no room for superiority complexes (vv 21–26). The monopolizing attempts of the Corinthian glossolalists seem to have prompted Paul to draw this comparison. Denial of the validity of the less spectacular charismatic functions of other members could mean no less than flagrant disregard for the grace character of one's own gift, as well as for the health of the whole body. Dunn has noted appropriately, "As the health of the whole depends on the proper functioning of each member, so the health of each member depends on the proper functioning of the whole."[189]

For Paul, therefore, the unity of the body was only guaranteed when members acknowledged the need for diversity of function, expressed in interdependence. Each of the gifts God had given into the Corinthian community was indispensable for the expression and maintenance of unity. But the diverse charismata which are essential to the unity of the body have, by the same token, a built-in limitation. Oscar Cullmann has noted this aspect and reasoned, "Where the Holy Spirit is at work, there exists no unity without multiplicity and no multiplicity without unity . . . ; he maintains their individuality while creating this unity —this is the paradox of the Holy Spirit in the New Testament."[190] The Corinthian dilemma, therefore, was not merely one of glossolalic monopoly, but one of disregard for the limitations of individual gifts. Their basic sin, Cullmann further declares, was against the charisma because they used the multiplicity of gifts as cause for division. "When unity is destroyed, charisma has ceased to be charisma."[191] Thus the functional purpose of charismatic endowment is fulfilled only when the well-being of the whole body is maintained as the sole reason for its existence in and for the community.

The Realm of the Gifts' Operation, 1 Cor 13

Chapter 13 does not represent Paul's plea for ἀγάπη as a charisma[192] to be preferred καθ᾽ ὑπερβολὴν ὁδόν from all others enumerated in ch 12, but ἀγάπη as the realm or context within which the charismata are practiced.[193] Contextually, the strategic placement between the statements of 12:31a and 14:1 in general and the intentional differentiation in 14:1 (strive for love but eagerly desire the spiritual gifts . . .) rule out the consideration of ἀγάπη as grace gift. Nor did Paul intend to pit love against gifts as a mode of the Christian life "which 'far surpasses' the life controlled by the charismata."[194]

"Love" and "gifts" must also be considered in their eschatological context. Thus, the "ode to divine love"[195] was Paul's means of instructing the Corinthians that charismatic functions would always remain temporal and imperfect. Their designated purpose was to provide the church with the various ministries necessary for its upbuilding during the age of the church. However, in the eschaton these charismata would no longer need to function because that which is perfect would have come (13:10).

All this does in no way diminish the fact that ἀγάπη itself belongs also to the work of the Spirit—perhaps its most elementary work.[196] If grace and charisma were given as part of the redemptive work of God to those believing, the same is true for ἀγάπη, "because God has poured out his love into our hearts by the Holy Spirit, whom he has given us" (Rom 5:5).

In the context of chs 12–14, however, Paul accepted "love" alone as the realm in which gifts were to function in their diversity. Outside ἀγάπη, any charismatic function was unable to upbuild the community. In fact, the opposite would be accomplished; the unity of the body would be destroyed because of divisiveness, and the growth of the body would be stunted.[197]

2 CORINTHIANS 1:11

After the profuse references to charismata and the rather detailed paraenesis concerning their desired function in I Corinthians and Romans, the sole instance in Paul's second letter to the Corinthian community (1:11) raises some questions. Had the problem which caused the apostle to write so extensively on the subject in the first place been solved? The silence of 2 Corinthians περὶ τῶν πνευματικῶν may lend implicit support to an affirmative answer. Or had Paul's occupation with the defense of his apostleship in his second letter prevented him from addressing charismatic giftedness further? Had the vision perhaps already begun to fade, as Dunn claimed of the Prison Epistles and of the Pastorals?[198] Any answer would be speculative; for Paul did not raise the issues at all.

From the context of vv 8–11 it seems evident that Paul's mention of τὸ εἰς ἡμᾶς χάρισμα did not reflect the technical usage accorded in Rom 12:6–8 and I Cor 12–14; that is, the reference here was not to one of the various enabling graces found in the above passages.[199] The available evidence allows for two possible identifications of the charisma.

One, the term may refer to the intercession which the Corinthians offered for Paul, according to v 11.[200] If that is correct, Paul held that the Corinthians' intercession was perhaps unparalleled and unsurpassed, and that his deliverance from a certain peril was the direct result of their charismatic intercession.

Two, the context strongly suggests that the charisma is actually the deliverance from a deadly peril, in answer to prayer.[201] The particular deliverance may have been that in Ephesus after the riot (Acts 19:23–41). In that case, the Pauline meaning of the term as "concretion of grace" is once again maintained. In this sense Barrett translates charisma as the "free gift of grace" with reference to "the act of rescue."[202] While the second view is better substantiated contextually, the first option must be left open as well. The diverse rendering of charisma in the English versions of 2 Cor 1:11 is illustrative of the ambiguity which exists at this point.[203]

1 TIMOTHY 4:14, 2 TIMOTHY 1:6

Two occurrences of the term charisma in the Pastorals are dealt with together because the historical occasion indicated in the context overlaps. The majority of interpreters accept deutero-Pauline authorship and a second-century date for 1 and 2 Timothy in view of the shift toward institutionalization in comparison to the main corpus of the Pauline writings.[204] This is generally considered standard for determining the significance of the concept of charisma in the passages to be considered. But even if one accepts authentic Pauline authorship and, therefore, a date of approximately AD 62–67[205] one may have to acknowledge the presence of certain changes in concept.

For one, the exhortation μὴ ἀμέλει τοῦ ἐν σοὶ χαρίσματος (1 Tim 4:14) seems to point to an internalizing of giftedness so that Timothy's charisma may be viewed as permanent. Paul's earlier correspondence left little doubt that charisma was a concrete action of God's grace when needed in, through, and for the community. This apparent internalization is coupled with the references to the reception of the gift through prophecy and through the laying on of hands by the presbytery (1 Tim 4:14), and/or through the laying on of hands by Paul (2 Tim 1:6). It is in this trend that Karol Gábriš finds the charismatic endowments institutionalized, for "they are no longer direct gifts of the Spirit of God."[206]

But the imposition of hands is not without precedent from the early beginnings of the church. In Acts 6:6 "the seven" were dedicated to their ministry by the laying on of hands by the apostles.[207] Paul and Barnabas were set apart and dedicated to the evangelization of the Gentiles by the same rite, performed by the Antiochian church leaders (Acts 13:3). It must be noted, however, that in both instances those dedicated to a certain task did not thereby receive a specific charisma; rather, the churches recognized and confirmed a particular enabling grace already evident. It is precisely this observation which causes some scholars to identify the laying of hands upon Timothy as the rite of ordination to the office of a presbyter.[208] Consequently, it is argued, the charisma of ordination to office probably was conferred upon Timothy in Ephesus.[209]

Against this line of argument, there is no textual or contextual evidence that the meaning of charisma has indeed changed from "grace gift" to "office." Several reasons may be adduced in support.

One, the emphasis in 1 Tim 4:14 is upon the verb ἀμελέω, so that Paul's purpose was to exhort his fellow minister "not to neglect the gift." In 2 Tim 1:6 Paul reminded Timothy even more strongly "to fan into flame the gift of God" (NIV). The verb ἀναζωπυρεῖν seems to intensify ἀμελέω.[210]

Two, the origin of the charisma has not changed; Paul still credits God as the giver of charismatic gifts. The objective gen. χάρισμα τοῦ θεοῦ (2 Tim 1:6) clearly points in that direction.[211]

Three, both references may recall Timothy's conversion experience in Lystra,[212] for justification, baptism in the Spirit, and charismatic enablement for service belong together. There is no reason, therefore, to take charisma in any other sense here than in the earlier Pauline letters. Charisma does not mean "office"; nor does it have the reduced significance of a mere possibility, "as foundational structure of the church."[213] Laying on of hands may more naturally be regarded as the external recognition of the gift bestowed by the Spirit. The accompanying prophetic utterance may also have confirmatory significance.

Four, both references may shed light on the human side of charismatic giftedness. In the Corinthian and Roman correspondence Paul's emphasis was singularly on the supernatural bestowal of gifts; and while in 1 and 2 Timothy this stress is still evident, though to a lesser degree, Timothy may not have been as assertive as Paul wanted him to be in the use of his charismatic ministry function. Both verbs, ἀμελέω and ἀναζωπυρεῖν, denote action for which Timothy was responsible. The challenge, then, may be not to leave God's gifts unused.

SUMMARY

The exegetical probe of the pericopes in which Paul used the term χάρισμα(τα) has shown in bold relief the great variety of its usage. He was able to designate most precisely and technically certain Spirit-given functions for the upbuilding of the community of faith (Rom 12:6–8,

1 Cor 12–14) as charismata, uniquely particularized in χαρίσματα ἰαμάτων (1 Cor 12:9, 28, 30). Paul also conceived of charisma in a very general manner as everything a person could experience as a result of God's χάρις, notably acquittal from guilt and, therefore, justification before God (Rom 5:15, 16), as well as the resultant gift of eternal life (Rom 6:23).

In Rom 1:11, 1 Cor 1:7, 1 Tim 4:14, and 2 Tim 1:6, the charismata are not directly linked to a particular category of gifts. Nevertheless, in each case the context may favor an allusion to one or to several grace gifts which Paul listed specifically, as in Rom 12:6–8 and in 1 Cor 12, or without the characteristic specification, as in 1 and 2 Timothy.

The broad sweep of charismatic endowment, for Paul, embraced every aspect of life. At one end of the spectrum, personal lifestyle (sexual continency or celibacy, 1 Cor 7:7) and particular personal experience (deliverance from a certain deadly peril, 2 Cor 1:11) had to be interpreted charismatically. Christian existence, then, could only be charismatic existence.

At the other end, God's redemptive purpose and plan for Israel as a nation, both from the historical and eschatological perspectives, also had to be classified as χαρίσματα τοῦ θεοῦ (Rom 11:29). Evidently this concept also expresses something about the uniqueness of God's covenantal relationship with his chosen people of the OT, as well as of the NT. It is not surprising, therefore, that Paul would understand the communities of believers as charismatic communities whose existence, growth, and well-being—in corporate worship and mission, in inspired utterance and gracious action on their behalf—were fully the expression of the manifold concretion of the grace of God.

Love was the only matrix within which Paul believed that charismatic endowment could truly fulfill the intended purpose, namely the upbuilding of the body. Whether directly or indirectly, all gifts would serve this end; for enabling graces divorced from the purpose of the upbuilding of the body express nothing more than sinful self-gratification. In fact, they would, according to Paul, no longer qualify as charismata since they were intended to express the community's unity through their diversity and interdependence.

In light of these findings, a definition of Paul's idea of charismata begins to crystallize. According to Paul's usage of the concept, charismata meant a diversity of experienced concretions of the grace of God, sovereignly bestowed by the Spirit upon members of the community of believers and functioning interdependently for the purpose of the upbuilding of the church in love, thereby demonstrating the Lordship of Christ. Charismatic endowment, then, is inevitably and integrally linked with service in and for the community. Recent interpreters of Paul have placed considerable emphasis upon this aspect. In the following chapter, therefore, the focus turns to grace gifts in terms of service.

NOTES

1. Käsemann, *Romans*, 19.

2. M. Black, *Romans*, NCeB, ed. M. Black (London: Marshall, Morgan & Scott, 1973), 41. Daniel Fraikin, " 'Charismes et ministères' à la lumière de 1 Cor. 12–14," *Église et Théologie* 9 (10, 1978): 457.

3. Fraikin, "Charismes et ministères," 457.

4. Against Oudersluys, "Charismatic Theology and the NT," 54.

5. So, most interpreters, e.g. Käsemann, *Romans*, 19; A. Nygren, *Commentary on Romans*, transl. C. C. Rasmussen (Philadelphia: Muhlenberg Press, 1949), 61; J. Murray, *The Epistle to the Romans*, 1 vol. ed., NICNT, ed. F. F. Bruce (Grand Rapids: Eerdmans, 1968), 22.

6. F. Godet, *Commentary on St. Paul's Epistle to the Romans*, transl. A. Cusin (Edinburgh: T. & T. Clark, 1980), 1:144; Murray, *Romans*, 22. However, Godet's insistence that the inserted dat. pron. ὑμῖν renders the adj. which follows more emphatic seems to give credence to a general concept of "charisma."

7. The use of the twofold pass. infin. and the construction τοῦτο δέ ἐστιν (only found here) are interesting in that they mellow Paul's zealous desire since he did not know the Roman community firsthand like he knew the Corinthian church. The one strengthening them, therefore, would be God himself who imparts the charisma, by his Spirit, in the first place.

8. H. W. Schmidt, *Der Brief des Paulus an die Römer*, THKNT, ed. D. E. Fascher (Berlin: Evangelische Verlagsanstalt, 1962), 6:25.

9. Hasenhüttl, *Charisma*, 131.

10. C. E. B. Cranfield, *A Critical and Exegetical Commentary on the Epistle to the Romans*, 6th rev. ed., ICC, ed. J. A. Emerton and C. E. B. Cranfield (Edinburgh: T. & T. Clark, 1975), 1:284.

11. For instance, C. K. Barrett, *A Commentary on the Epistle to the Romans*, HNTC, ed. H. Chadwick (New York: Harper & Row, 1957), 113–14.

12. Murray, *Romans*, 195–96.

13. So, AV, NASB, RBV. On the other hand, the parallelism is affirmed by RSV and NIV which translate all three terms consistently as "free gift" and "gift," respectively.

14. Δώρημα occurs only here (v 16) in the Pauline corpus and elsewhere in the NT only in Jas 1:17. Parry's claim that δώρημα is the result or concrete effect of both χάρις and δωρεά is an unfounded differentiation. R. St. John Parry, *The Epistle of Paul the Apostle to the Romans*, CGTC (Cambridge: University Press, 1921), 87. The term δωρεά occurs only twice in Romans (5:15,

17). This fact does not make for substantial support of a distinction from χάρισμα.

Brockhaus regards the Pauline use of χάρισμα and δώρημα as the closest parallel to Alciphron III, 17:4, where both terms also appear synonymously. But his conclusion that χάρισμα, therefore, does not exceed the Hellenistic frame of reference of "gift" or "present" cannot be sustained contextually.

15. Käsemann, *Romans*, 139–40. See the NEB's similar rendering.

16. See J. Denney, *St. Paul's Epistle to the Romans*, ExpGT, ed. W. Robertson Nicholl (Grand Rapids: Eerdmans, 1956), 2:629; Cranfield, *Romans*, 1:284. In 2 Cor 9:15 Paul uses δωρεά to express God's gift to humanity in Christ.

17. Dunn, *Jesus and the Spirit*, 206; Parry, *Romans*, 87; Barrett, *Romans*, 114.

18. Brockhaus, *Charisma und Amt*, 132. Piepkorn, "Χάρισμα in the NT," 370, maintains that the idea of acquittal is implicit in the noun "charisma" since the cognate verb χαρίζομαι is used to describe the freeing of an offender (Acts 3:14) and thus generally means "to forgive" (2 Cor 2:7, 10; 12:13; Eph 4:32; Col 2:13; 3:13). Yet, cf. Rom 8:32 and 1 Cor 2:12 where the verb means "to give freely" or "to give graciously."

19. Murray, *Romans*, 196; Parry, *Romans*, 86.

20. Some interpreters treat χάρισμα and ὀψώνια as parallel expressions, following the lead of Tertullian who translated ὀψώνια with the Latin *donativum*. Ὀψώνια means "wage," "ration" paid to the soldier. Consequently, χάρισμα means extraordinary wage of grace. In favor of this position, see H. W. Heidland, *TDNT*, s.v. "ὀψώνια;" Schmidt, *Römer*, 118; Black, *Romans*, 99.

Against this view and espousing contrast, see Cranfield, *Romans*, 1:329–30; Murray, *Romans*, 237–38; C. H. Dodd, *The Epistle of Paul to the Romans*, MNTC, ed. J. Moffatt (New York: Harper & Brothers, 1932), 99; Hasenhüttl, *Charisma*, 330; Brockhaus, *Charisma und Amt*, 132–33.

21. The gen. is to be taken as subjective, i.e. wages which sin, as general, pays, rather than wages paid for sin (objective). See Cranfield, *Romans*, 1:329.

22. Käsemann, "Ministry and Community," 64.

23. Barrett, *Romans*, 134; Karl Kertelge, *Gemeinde und Amt im NT* (Munich: Kösel-Verlag, 1972) 104–5.

24. J. R. Williams, *The Pentecostal Reality* (Plainfield, NJ: Logos International, 1972), 17.

25. Against Koenig, *Charismata*, 97.

26. See Dunn's excellent discussion in *Jesus and the Spirit*, 260–65.

27. Dunn, *Jesus and the Spirit*, 207; Barrett, *Romans*, 225; Parry, *Romans*, 150. Käsemann's notion that χαρίσματα and κλῆσις are synonymous must be rejected on the basis of the conjunctive construction as well as for contextual reasons, "Ministry and Community," 65. Schmidt's attempt to subordinate "calling" as the most important among the grace gifts is unacceptable for the same reasons; *Römer*, 202.

28. Brockhaus, *Charisma und Amt*, 134.

29. Dunn, *Jesus and the Spirit*, 207.

30. By no means does this imply unqualified universalism. But it does

take Paul seriously at the point of 11:26, "And so all Israel will be saved."
There would yet be a significant turning back to God on Israel's part, although
the apostle remained silent about the timetable of this event. See J.
Moltmann's chapter on "The Church and Israel," in *The Church in the Power of the Spirit*,
136–50, and B. Corley, "Jews, the Future, and God," *SWJT* 19 (Fall 1976):
42–56.

31. E.g., Brockhaus, *Charisma*, 139; Kertelge, *Gemeinde und Amt im
NT*, 104–8.

32. So, Black, *Romans*, 153, who omits v 6 which forms the basis for a
proper understanding of vv 7 and 8; F. F. Bruce, *The Epistle of Paul to the
Romans*, Tyn, ed. R. V. G. Tasker (Grand Rapids: Eerdmans, 1978 [repr.]),
228.

33. J. Gnilka, "Geistliches Amt und Gemeinde nach Paulus," in *Foi et
Salut Selon S. Paul (Épître au Romains 1:16)*, AnBib (Rome: Institut Biblique
Pontifical, 1970), 42:237.

34. See Brockhaus' excellent discussion of the paraenetic character and
function of χάρισμα in Rom 12, *Charisma*, 193–202.

35. Murray, *Romans*, 120–21; Barrett, *Romans*, 237; W. Sanday and
A. C. Headlam, *A Critical and Exegetical Commentary on the Epistle to the
Romans*, 5th ed., ICC, eds. S. R. Driver, A. Plummer, and C. A. Briggs
(Edinburgh: T. & T. Clark, 1902), 356; and others.

36. D. Hill, *New Testament Prophecy*, in *The New Testament Theological
Library*, ed. P. Toon (Atlanta: John Knox, 1979), 122–23. He asserts that
"when they are taken together, παράκλησις, παραμυθία, and οἰκοδομή provide the nearest approach in Paul's letters to a definition of the prophetic function,"
123.

37. Hence Käsemann's vague suggestion that the teacher is "not radically
distinguished from the prophet," *Romans*, 342. H. Schürmann argues that
prophecy holds a singularly preeminent place while διακονία summarizes the
subsequent group of ministries, "Die Geistlichen Gnadengaben in den
Paulinischen Gemeinden," in *Ursprung and Gestalt: Erörterungen und
Besinnungen zum Neuen Testament* (Düsseldorf: Patmos-Verlag, 1970), 255.

38. Against Barrett, *Romans*, 237, and Käsemann, *Romans*, 341.

39. G. Friedrich, "προφήτης, κ.τ.λ.," *TDNT*, 6:850; also R. H.
Culpepper, *Evaluating the Charismatic Movement: A Theological and Biblical
Appraisal* (Valley Forge: Judson Press, 1977), 113–15; Hasenhüttl, *Charisma*,
185.

40. H. Schürmann, "Die Geistlichen Gnadengaben," 253.

41. See Murray, *Romans*, 122; Kertelge, *Gemeinde und Amt*, 109, and
esp. 120. Ulrich Müller maintains that prophetic preaching was characteristic of
earliest Christianity and its communal gatherings, *Prophetie und Predigt im
Neuen Testament* (Gütersloh: Gütersloher Verlagshaus Gerd Mohn, 1975) 239.
Against the identification of prophecy with preaching, see M. Green, *I Believe
in the Holy Spirit* (Grand Rapids: Eerdmans, 1975), 171; Dunn, *Jesus and the
Spirit*, 228.

42. So, Schürmann, "Die Geistlichen Gnadengaben," 253.

43. H. Schlier, *Der Römerbrief*, HTKNT, ed. A. Wikenhauser, A. Vögtle,

and R. Schnackenburg (Freiburg: Verlag Herder, 1977), 6:369.

44. Dunn, *Jesus and the Spirit*, 228.

45. Spontaneity is not to be understood as lack of control or disorder; nor in parallelism of the Hellenistic enthusiasm.

46. Murray, *Romans*, 122–23.

47. This constitutes the only occurrence of ἀναλογία in NT literature and generally is translated "proportion." If ἀναλογίαν τῆς πίστεως is taken as objective gen., the meaning could be something like "analogy of faith." Paul would then have used πίστις as *fides quae creditur*, similar to the usage in Gal 1:23 where πίστις is the object of εὐαγγελίζεσθαι or πορθεῖν. For this view, see R. Bultmann, "Πιστεύω, κ.τ.λ.," *TDNT*, 6:213; Schlier, *Römer*, 370, carries the argument to its logical conclusion. Faith then becomes a set of principles, dogmas, or traditions belonging to a church. The other possibility, espoused by a majority of interpreters, is to take ἀναλογίαν τῆς πίστεως as subjective gen., translating as "proportion of faith." In this case, faith is understood as *fides qua creditur*; Murray, *Romans*, 123; Barrett, *Romans*, 238; Sanday and Headlam, *Romans*, 356–57.

48. Murray, *Romans*, 124.

49. Hill, *NT Prophecy*, 119.

50. Dunn, *Jesus and the Spirit*, 233.

51. The same meaning also emerges from the only non-Pauline passage, 1 Pet 4:10; cf. H. W. Beyer, "διακονέω, κ.τ.λ.," *TDNT*, 2:86; Hasenhüttl, *Charisma*, 159.

52. Yet, Siegfried Grossmann seems to imply precisely this when he asserts that "διακονία is almost a universal gift for everyday living, for it is concerned with everything necessary to a person's daily life," *Charisma: The Gifts of the Spirit*, transl. S. Wiesmann (Wheaton, IL: Key Publishers, Inc., 1971), 29.

53. Murray, *Romans*, 123–24. Perhaps the singular reading of διδασκαλία in A, instead of διδάσκων, following the preponderance of the MSS, in 12:8, suggests that fifth-century copyists understood διακονία as ministry of the Word; on the other hand, the reading ὁ διακόνων by ℵ², 1241, 1506 p.c., may represent an attempt to streamline Paul's use of the participles following προφητεία, thereby setting up prophecy as the χάρισμα par excellence.

54. Beyer, *TDNT*, 2:87–88; Murray, *Romans*, 124; Barrett, *Romans*, 238.

55. Perhaps Käsemann's suggestion of "assistance of any kind" does justice to a "both-and" approach, *Romans*, 342; see also Schlier, *Römer*, 370. The notion of the existence of a diaconate, or office, cannot be supported from the threefold usage of the noun διακονία in Romans, nor from the Corinthian correspondence; against Käsemann, *Romans*, 342; Murray, *Romans*, 124. Even Barrett's idea that in 12:7 διακονία is "already on the way to becoming a technical term" is too narrowly conceived; if it is a technical term, in what way? as "ministry of the Word," as "act of service," or as "office"?

56. Barrett, *Romans*, 238. Consequently, he finds it difficult to distinguish between "preaching" and "teaching."

57. Käsemann, *Romans*, 342.

58. Dunn, *Jesus and the Spirit*, 237–38, italics are his. Cf. Col 3:16

where, among other things, "teaching" expresses the word of Christ dwelling in them.

59. Dunn, *Jesus and the Spirit*, 237–38.

60. Käsemann, *Romans*, 342.

61. H. Schürmann provides the best and clearest chart of the Pauline lists of χαρίσματα in "Die Geistlichen Gnadengaben," 250–51. Regrettably, he omits διακονία from his list of Rom 12:6–8, thereby exposing his own interpretive bias.

62. See also 2 Cor 10:1; 1 Thes 4:1; Phil 4:2; Eph 4:1; and others.

63. O. Schmitz, "παρακαλέω, παράκλησις," *TDNT*, 5:796–99.

64. Although "comfort" or "consolation" translates the noun παραμυθία in 1 Cor 14:3.

65. So, Murray, *Romans*, 125. The variation in emphasis is also evident in the translations; AV, RSV, NASB translate "exhort"; NIV translates "encourage." NEB goes its own way with "the gift of stirring speech."

66. Schmitz, *TDNT*, 5:796.

67. Schlier, *Römer*, 371; Käsemann, *Romans*, 342.

68. Sanday and Headlam, *Romans*, 357; Schlier, *Römer*, 371; Dunn, *Jesus and the Spirit*, 250.

69. Against Käsemann, *Romans*, 342. Schlier, after correctly noting the meaning intended here, follows the lead of Käsemann and moves it into the category of institutionalized functions. He detects in the μεταδιδούς the "distributor of collected funds or more generally, the public assistance officer," *Römer*, 371. Similarly, Koenig suggests that Paul's mind lingered on the collection for the church in Jerusalem. And since he called it a χάρις, a gracious work, in 2 Cor 8:6, 7, 19, he may have conceived of this type of unselfish giving as a χάρισμα. But that does not answer the more basic question of whether this was indeed Paul's intent in Rom 12:8; John Koenig, "From Mystery to Ministry: Paul as Interpreter of Charismatic Gifts," *USQR* 33 (Spring 1978): 170.

70. Murray, *Romans*, 126; Schlier, *Römer*, 372.

71. John Knox, "The Epistle to the Romans: Introduction and Exegesis," in IB, ed. G. A. Buttrick (New York: Abingdon, 1954), 9:585; Sanday and Headlam, *Romans*, 357.

72. Barrett, *Romans*, 238–39. He comments further on the meaning, "being without arrière-pensée in one's gift."

73. Knox, "Romans," 585–86; Parry, *Romans*, 163; Dunn, *Jesus and the Spirit*, 250.

74. 1 Cor 13:3 serves as a sobering reminder that giving per se does not necessarily merit the distinction of charismatic endowment.

75. So, the NIV, NASB, NEB: "leadership"; RSV: "giving aid"; AV: "to rule."

76. Murray, *Romans*, 126; Schlier, *Römer*, 372; Barrett, *Romans*, 239. Käsemann carries the idea too far in suggesting that προϊστάμενος points to "various organizational tasks, including the founding of house-churches and the settlement of disputes," *Romans*, 342. Barrett notes more correctly that "it does not describe any office with precision but refers to a function exercised by

many," *Romans*, 239.

77. Dunn, *Jesus and the Spirit*, 250–51; Schlier, *Römer*, 372.

78. Dunn, *Jesus and the Spirit*, 251.

79. Dunn maintains that "zest" best captures the sense because it is an expression of the community's vitality.

80. Schlier, *Römer*, 372; Murray, *Romans*, 127. If these functions overlap, as Dunn readily concurs, one wonders why he draws the arbitrary distinction that μεταδιδούς probably meant shared food, possessions, and especially clothing, while ἐλεῶν meant primarily the giving of financial aid, *Jesus and the Spirit*, 426, n. 270. With overlapping functions, the resources used in carrying out this function likely also overlapped.

81. From ἱλαρότητι derives the English noun "hilarity"; in the Gk. NT it occurs only here.

82. RSV translates ἐν παντὶ λόγῳ as "with all speech," and the NIV as "in all speaking." The idea may well be that of various forms of inspired speech which Paul—perhaps deliberately—declined to define more specifically.

83. Against F. W. Grosheide who pleads for a general meaning of the term. He assumes that Paul probably did not yet possess all the information which precipitated his dealing with the πνευματικά in chs 12–14, and that there is no indication that the Corinthians had already received all the special gifts of 12:8–10 at that time. But Grosheide's reasoning ignores entirely the context in which 1:7 is couched; his conclusions do not reflect exegetical categories as much as his own presupposition that these "special gifts" ceased at the end of the apostolic era, *Commentary on the First Epistle to the Corinthians*, NICNT, ed. N. B. Stonehouse (Grand Rapids: Eerdmans, 1953), 29–30.

84. J. W. MacGorman, *Layman's Bible Book Commentary. Romans, 1 Corinthians* (Nashville: Broadman, 1980), 20:101; Brockhaus, *Charisma*, 135–36.

85. Ὥστε with the infinitive indicates a result clause; thus Paul conveyed a fact, not a hypothetical situation. See G. G. Findlay, *St. Paul's First Epistle to the Corinthians* ExpGT, ed. W. Robertson Nicholl (Grand Rapids: Eerdmans, n.d.), 2:760. See also W. J. Bartling, "Congregation of Christ: A Charismatic Body; an Exegetical Study of 1 Cor. 12," *CTM* 40 (2, 1969): 69.

86. C. K. Barrett, *A Commentary on the First Epistle to the Corinthians*, HNTC, ed. H. Chadwick (New York: Harper & Row, 1968), 38, this writer's italics.

87. Hans Conzelmann, *1 Corinthians*, 28. Similarly, H-D. Wendland, *Die Briefe an die Korinther*, 8th ed., NTD, ed. P. Althaus and G. Friedrich (Göttingen: Vandenhoeck & Ruprecht, 1962), 12.

88. Priebe, "Charismatic Gifts and Christian Existence," 31; cf. esp. chs 3 and 5 in J. C. Hurd, Jr., *The Origin of 1 Corinthians* (New York: Seabury, 1965), 61–95, 114–209.

89. Hasenhüttl, *Charisma*, 138.

90. A. Robertson and A. Plummer, *A Critical and Exegetical Commentary on the First Epistle of St. Paul to the Corinthians*, 2d ed., ICC, eds. S. R. Driver, A. Plummer, and C. A. Briggs (Edinburgh: T. & T. Clark, 1914, repr. 1963), 136; Wendland, *Korinther*, 51; Grosheide, *1 Corinthians*, 159; Oudersluys, "Charismatic Theology and the NT," 54.

91. MacGorman, *Romans, 1 Corinthians*, 120; similarly, Wendland, *Korinther*, 51.

92. W. F. Orr and J. A. Walther, *1 Corinthians*, AB, eds. F. M. Cross, R. E. Brown, and J. C. Greenfield (Garden City, NY: Doubleday & Co., 1976), 207; J. Ruef, *Paul's First Letter to Corinth*, WPC, ed. D. E. Nineham (Philadelphia: Westminster, 1977), 55; L. Morris, *The First Epistle of Paul to the Corinthians*, Tyn, ed. R. V. G. Tasker (Grand Rapids: Eerdmans, 1958), 108. The description of marriage as charisma may have originated in Alexandria; the earliest mention stems from Clement of Alexandria, and Origen followed suit. Cf. Findlay, *1 Corinthians*, 824; Robertson and Plummer, *1 Corinthians*, 136.

93. So, Moltmann, *Church in the Power of the Spirit*, 241; W. J. Hollenweger, "Creator Spiritus," *Theology* 81 (1, 1978): 33. Yet, if parenthood is an implied charisma, why not also extend the implication to abstention from parenthood?

94. Moltmann, *Church in the Power of the Spirit*, 296.

95. Findlay, *1 Corinthians*, 824; Conzelmann, *1 Corinthians*, 118; Wendland, *Korinther*, 51; D. H. Lietzmann and W. G. Kümmel, *An die Korinther 1 & 2*, 5th ed., HNT, ed. G. Bornkamm (Tübingen: J. C. B. Mohr, 1969), 9:30. Lietzmann is probably the most outspoken critic of the inclusion of marriage as charisma.

96. Hasenhüttl, *Charisma*, 156; see also Brockhaus, *Charisma und Amt*, 136–37.

97. This interpretation has been suggested and vigorously defended by Sister Evangéline, "The Monastic Life: A Charismatic Life in the Church," *The Ecumenical Review* 31 (7, 1979): 273–78. Her conclusion deserves mention here: "To assert that the monastic life is a universal charism is not to say that everyone should become a monk or a nun, or that monks or nuns should live as if they were not monks or nuns. But it means that alongside the parishes and together with them, monasteries have a responsibility for the Church because of the richness of their experience," 278. It is difficult, for this writer, to grasp how the internalizing of monasticism—Sister Evangéline calls it "interiorized monasticism"—could still be understood as a charism of continence.

98. See Conzelmann, *1 Corinthians*, 204; Lietzmann, *1 Korinther*, 60; F. F. Bruce, *1 & 2 Corinthians*, NCBC, ed. M. Black (Grand Rapids: Eerdmans, 1971), 117; H. L. Goudge, *The First Epistle to the Corinthians*, WC, ed. W. Lock (London: Methuen & Co., 1903), 108; Hurd, *Origin of 1 Corinthians*, 73; and most interpreters. For the attempt to dispute the unity and, more particularly, to displace ch 13 from the present position to the end of ch 14, see W. Schmithals, *Die Gnosis in Korinth* (Göttingen: Vandenhoeck & Ruprecht, 1969), 89 (ET *Gnosticism in Corinth; An Investigation of the Letters to the Corinthians*, transl. J. E. Steely (Nashville: Abingdon, 1971); Barrett, *1 Corinthians*, 314–15.

99. The seminal study to be consulted on the background of 1 Corinthians still is J. C. Hurd, Jr., *The Origin of 1 Corinthians*.

100. F. F. Bruce suggests that since the resurrection issue is not introduced by this standard formula—nor are the issues contained in ch 11—perhaps

Paul was given this information orally by the three Corinthian travelers Stephanas, Fortunatus, and Achaicus, *1 & 2 Corinthians*, 24.

101. Schmithals, *Gnosticism in Corinth*; see also his article, "Geister-fahrung als Christuserfahrung," in *Erfahrung und Theologie des Heiligen Geistes*, eds. C. Heitmann and H. Mühlen (Hamburg: Agentur des Rauhen Hauses, and Munich: Kösel-Verlag, 1974), 101–17; Wendland, *Korinther*, 92.

102. J. MacArthur, *The Charismatics: A Doctrinal Perspective* (Grand Rapids: Zondervan, 1978), 107–8. MacArthur fails to present an objective appraisal, and does not take sufficient account of the recent balanced scholarly approaches both from outside and from within the charismatic movement.

103. E.g., J. W. MacGorman, *The Gifts of the Spirit. An Exposition of 1 Corinthians 12–14* (Nashville: Broadman, 1974), 13–17; Brockhaus, *Charisma und Amt*, 150–56.

104. Ellis, "Spiritual Gifts in the Pauline Community," 130–31.

105. Oudersluys, "Charismatic Theology and the New Testament," 54.

106. G. Theissen, *The Social Setting of Pauline Christianity: Essays on Corinth*, ed. and transl. and with an introduction by J. H. Schütz (Philadelphia: Fortress, 1982), esp. 69–102.

107. Hollenweger, *Conflict in Corinth*, 3–35, 65–74.

108. Bartling, "Congregation of Christ," 69.

109. The majority of commentators opt for the neut. reading, translating "spiritual gifts"; e.g., Conzelmann, *1 Corinthians*, 204; Wendland, *Korinther*, 92; Robertson and Plummer, *1 Corinthians*, 259; Findlay, *1 Corinthians*, 885. Generally this conclusion is reached on the basis of 14:1 where the neut. is undisputed.

110. Bruce, *1 & 2 Corinthians*, 116; Bartling, "Congregation of Christ," 68; Ellis, "Spiritual Gifts in the Pauline Community," 128, suggests that with that term Paul may have had both in mind: gifts of inspired utterance and men who exercised such gifts.

111. Barrett, *1 Corinthians*, 278; see also Morris, *1 Corinthians*, 166.

112. Bartling, "Congregation of Christ," 68.

113. Dunn, *Jesus and the Spirit*, 207.

114. So, Käsemann, "Ministry and Community," 66; D. L. Baker, "Interpretation of 1 Corinthians 12–14" *EvQ* 46 (10, 1974): 226.

115. Baker, "Interpretation of 1 Cor. 12–14," 230.

116. Ruef, *1 Corinthians*, 126.

117. See Käsemann, "Ministry and Community," 66; D. W. B. Robinson, "Charismata versus Pneumatika; Paul's Method of Discussion," *The Reformed Theological Review* 31 (5, 1972): 49–55. The notion that πνευματικά referred only to inspired speech (i.e., prophecy, speaking in tongues, or discernment) cannot be substantiated from 1 Cor 12:8–10 where Paul listed a number of gifts not associated with inspired speech. When Paul referred to the πνευματικά in 14:1 and singled out prophecy as very desirable, he did so for reasons of corrective instruction. Paul cited other gifts also; namely interpretation of tongues (14:5, 13, 26–28), revelation, knowledge, teaching (14:6, 26). If these are incidental to Paul's main argument, one runs the danger of relegating ch 14 to Pauline polemics—hardly a balanced view. Against Baker, "Interpretation of

1 Cor 12–14," 228. Ellis, "Spiritual Gifts in the Pauline Communities," 129, restricts πνευματικά to "gifts of inspired perception, verbal proclamation and/or its interpretation."

118. T. Holtz, "Das Kennzeichen des Geistes; 1 Kor. 12:1–3," *NTS* 18 (4, 1972): 373–74. See also E. Schweizer, "What is the Holy Spirit: A Study in Biblical Theology," transl. G. W. S. Knowles, in *Conflicts About the Holy Spirit*, eds. H. Küng, and J. Moltmann, *Concilium—Religion in the Seventies* (New York: Seabury, 1979), 128:xiii.

119. Holtz, "Das Kennzeichen des Geistes," 375.

120. Ruef, *1 Corinthians*, 126; cf. also Wendland, *Korinther*, 93.

121. Bruce, *1 & 2 Corinthians*, 118.

122. P. E.-B. Allo, *Saint Paul: Première Épître aux Corinthiens*, 2nd ed., EBib (Paris: J. Gabalda & Co., 1956), 321–22. Barrett, *1 Corinthians*, 280, follows Allo's example.

123. Brockhaus, *Charisma und Amt*, 160–61.

124. H. Saake, "Pneumatologia Paulina: zur Katholizität der Problematik des Charisma," *Catholica* 26 (7, 1972): 217, sets the passage of 12:4–11 into a broader triadic contextual pattern. It serves a double function. Not only does it pick up Paul's main concern again from vv 1–3, it also is part of the triadic relationship and context of πνεῦμα (4), κύριος (5), and θεός (6a), and is paralleled again by *pneuma* (4; i.e., 7–11), Christ (12–27), and God (28–30).

125. MacGorman, *Romans, 1 Corinthians*, 137.

126. Parry, *1 Corinthians*, 173.

127. Lietzmann, *Korinther*, 61.

128. Conzelmann, *1 Corinthians*, 207.

129. So, Brockhaus, *Charisma und Amt*, 139.

130. Schürmann, "Geistliche Gnadengaben," 244. Lietzmann restricts —indeed, misunderstands—the parallel usage of διακονία with χαρίσματα here by claiming that the former is further clarified in v 28 by ἀντιλήμψεις and κυβερνήσεις, *Korinther*, 61.

131. Richard C. Oudersluys, "The Purpose of Spiritual Gifts," *Reformed Review* 28 (Spring 1975): 217.

132. Orr and Walther, *1 Corinthians*, 281.

133. Heinrich Schlier, "Herkunft, Ankunft und Wirkungen des Heiligen Geistes im Neuen Testament," in *Erfahrung und Theologie des Heiligen Geistes*, eds. C. Heitmann and H. Mühlen (Hamburg: Agentur des Rauhen Hauses, and Munich: Kösel-Verlag, 1974), 127.

134. Barrett, *1 Corinthians*, 284.

135. E.g., Robert L. Brandt, *Spiritual Gifts, The Christian Service Series*, no. 15 (Brussels: International Correspondence Institute, 1980), see esp. the table of contents, p. 5. But see Stanley Horton, *What the Bible Says About the Holy Spirit* (Springfield, MO: Gospel Publishing House, 1976), 208–9, for a better, more balanced perspective.

136. Krister Stendahl, "Glossolalia—The New Testament Evidence," in *Paul Among the Jews and Gentiles* (Philadelphia: Fortress, 1976), 112, repr. from *The Charismatic Movement*, ed. M. P. Hamilton (Grand Rapids: Eerdmans, 1975).

In fact, it would be wrong to attribute to Paul even a conscious, let alone deliberate, organization of charismata in 12:8–10, as Bruce endeavors to do in *1 & 2 Corinthians*, 119. This is not to deny the facility of grouping together the gifts, as Michael Green has done, for instance. He finds three groups given: (1) Gifts to know (wisdom, knowledge, discerning of spirits), (2) gifts to do (faith, healings, miracles), and (3) gifts to say (prophecy, tongues, and interpretation); *I Believe in the Holy Spirit*, 161. Similarly, Conzelmann, *1 Corinthians*, 209.

137. For a full discussion of what the Corinthian concept of σοφία might have been, see Dunn, *Jesus and the Spirit*, 217–21; Hasenhüttl, *Charisma*, 140–44; Barrett, *1 Corinthians*, 67–68.

138. Against Grosheide, *1 Corinthians*, 285.

139. Hasenhüttl, *Charisma*, 143.

140. Schürmann, "Geistliche Gnadengaben," 256; Banks, *Paul's Idea of Community*, 96.

141. Dunn, *Jesus and the Spirit*, 217–18.

142. Banks, *Paul's Idea of Community*, 96.

143. Schürmann, "Geistliche Gnadengaben," 256.

144. Wendland, *Korinther*, 94; Conzelmann, *1 Corinthians*, 209. He maintains, "Both mean the gift of speaking instructively."

145. Following Hasenhüttl, *Charisma*, 144.

146. Dunn, *Jesus and the Spirit*, 211; Barrett, *1 Corinthians*, 285.

147. So, Grossmann, *Charisma*, 70–72.

148. Conzelmann, *1 Corinthians*, 209. Joseph Ratzinger postulates that the Corinthians had their own triad of gifts, namely σοφία, γνῶσις, πίστις. Opposite theirs, Paul established his own; namely πίστις, ἐλπίς, ἀγάπη; as well as his own catalogue of charisms which he introduced with the triad of ἀπόστολοι, προφῆται, διδάσκαλοι. The Pauline double triad was directed against the Corinthian fanaticism. But then Ratzinger dismisses contextual considerations and arbitrarily distinguishes, "As the differing 'powerful deeds' (glossolalia, gifts of healing, etc.) are tied to the standard of the upbuilding of the church, so the actual word charisms (wisdom, knowledge, prophecy) are tied to the standard of faith," "Bemerkungen zur Frage der Charismen in der Kirche," in *Die Zeit Jesu. FS für Heinrich Schlier*, eds. G. Bornkamm and K. Rahner (Freiburg: Verlag Herder KG, 1970), 264–66.

149. Hasenhüttl, *Charisma*, 148. Dunn's statement, "The charisma is not a healing power which is effective for all [sorts of] illnesses; it is *the* actual healing itself," *Jesus and the Spirit*, 211 (italics his), tends to stop short of carrying through his otherwise constant insistence that the charisma is always the "*gracious activity (ἐνέργημα) of God through a man*," 254.

150. See MacGorman, *Gifts of the Spirit*, 38; Barrett, *1 Corinthians*, 285; Banks, *Paul's Idea of Community*, 96.

151. Hasenhüttl, *Charisma*, 146–47.

152. Barrett, *1 Corinthians*, 286.

153. Kertelge, *Gemeinde und Amt im Neuen Testament*, 119–21. He sees "general prophetic function" in operation in 1 Cor 11:4–5, whereas in chs 12–14 the tendency to institutionalize prophecy is evident. See also Hasenhüttl, *Charisma*, 193, where he ascribes to the prophets an "independence which does not permit their subjection to any other group."

154. Ellis, "Spiritual Gifts in the Pauline Community," 129–31.

155. U. B. Müller, *Prophetie und Predigt im Neuen Testament. Form-geschichtliche Untersuchungen zur urchristlichen Prophetie* (Gütersloh: Gütersloher Verlagshaus Gerd Mohn, 1975), see index. Cf. also Wendland, *Korinther*, 95; Kertelge, *Gemeinde und Amt im NT*, 12.

156. Dunn, *Jesus and the Spirit*, 228.

157. Hill, *NT Prophecy*, 132–33; W. Grudem, *The Gift of Prophecy in 1 Corinthians* (Washington, DC: University Press of America, 1982); H. Freiherr von Campenhausen, *Ecclesiastical Authority and Spiritual Power in the Church of the First Three Centuries*, transl. J. A. Baker (Stanford, CA: Stanford University Press, 1969), 61. However, stressing discontinuity is Hasenhüttl, *Charisma*, 193.

158. Hill, *NT Prophecy*, 135; Hasenhüttl, *Charisma*, 189. The issue of authority expressed by the charismata will be further explored in chapter 5.

159. G. Dautzenberg, *Urchristliche Prophetie: Ihre Forschung, ihre Voraussetzungen im Judentum und ihre Struktur im ersten Korintherbrief*, BWANT, 6th ed., eds. S. Herrmann and K. H. Rengstorf (Stuttgart: Verlag W. Kohlhammer, 1975), 4:301; also "Zum religionsgeschichtlichen Hintergrund der διάκρισις πνευμάτων (1 Kor 12:10)," *BZ* 15 (1, 1971): 93–104. See also R. P. Brown, "Gifts of the Holy Spirit," *Reformed Review* 28 (Spring 1975): 176, who defines similarly, "[Prophecy is] the ability to see clearly into a subject and discern the right and wrong of it."

160. See Müller's excellent rebuttal of Dautzenberg's view of prophecy, *Prophetie und Predigt*, 27–28; as well as Wayne Grudem's response to Dautzenberg's article, "Response to Gerhard Dautzenberg on 1 Cor. 12:10," *BZ* 22 (7, 1978): 253–70.

161. See MacGorman, *Gifts of the Spirit*, 80–109; Dunn, *Jesus and the Spirit*, 229–33; Green, *I Believe in the Holy Spirit*, 170–71.

162. Dunn, *Jesus and the Spirit*, 233. See also the able treatment of Gérard Thérrien, *Le Discernment dans les Écrits Pauliniens*, EBib (Paris: J. Gabalda & Co., 1973), 76.

163. J. D. G. Dunn, "Prophetic 'I'-Sayings and the Jesus Tradition: the importance of testing prophetic utterances in early Christianity," *NTS* 24 (1, 1978): 175–98; Bruce, *1 & 2 Corinthians*, 119; Barrett, *1 Corinthians*, 286, shows the same tendency. The reference to οἱ ἄλλοι διακρινέτωσαν in 14:29 is not conclusive evidence for Dunn's position either. Οἱ ἄλλοι could be interpreted to mean the other prophets present; more likely, however, it may embrace all other participants in the gathering. In 1 Thes 5:21 the hortatory δοκιμάζετε likewise applied to the entire congregation.

164. Dautzenberg, "Zum religionsgeschichtlichen Hintergrund," 104.

165. Ruef, *1 Corinthians*, 129; Lietzmann, *Korinther*, 61; MacGorman, *Gifts of the Spirit*, 42. Wendland, *Korinther*, 95, thinks that such discernment is only necessary "when ecstatics speak." See also Thérrien, *Le Discernment*, 60.

166. Dunn, "Prophetic 'I'-Sayings," 189–90; and his more elaborate treatment of the same in *Jesus and the Spirit*, 293–97.

167. Hurd, *Origin of 1 Corinthians*, 72; Brockhaus, *Charisma und Amt*, 150–53.

168. Grossmann, *Charisma*, 77–78; Johannes Behm, s.v. "γλῶσσα,"

TDNT, 1:720.

169. As in Acts 2:4ff; e.g., D. Bridge and D. Phypers, *Spiritual Gifts and the Church* (Downers Grove, IL: Inter Varsity Press, 1973).

170. As in 1 Cor 13:2; e.g., Barrett, *1 Corinthians*, 299–300; Dunn, *Jesus and the Spirit*, 244; Wendland, *Korinther*, 119.

171. BAGD, 161; Barrett, *1 Corinthians*, 286; see also the NEB translation, "ecstatic utterance."

172. E.g., O. Cullmann, "La prière selon les épîtres pauliniennes: conference donnée à l'Université d'Athène le 11 Mai 1978," *TZ* 35 (3, 1979): 90–101.

173. Hollenweger, *The Pentecostals*, 344.

174. Dunn, *Jesus and the Spirit*, 248; Green, *I Believe in the Holy Spirit*, 167.

175. Behm, s.v. "ἑρμηνεύω, κ.τ.λ.," *TDNT*, 2:665; Banks, *Paul's Idea of Community*, 96.

176. A. C. Thiselton, "The 'interpretation' of tongues: a new suggestion in the light of Greek usage in Philo and Josephus," *JTS*, n.s., 30 (4, 1979): 15–36.

177. K. H. Rengstorf, s.v. "ἀποστέλλω, κ.τ.λ.," *TDNT*, 1:421; Barrett, *1 Corinthians*, 293.

178. See Hasenhüttl, *Charisma*, 165–67.

179. See E. Lohse, "Die Gemeinde und ihre Ordnung bei den Synoptikern und bei Paulus," in *Jesus und Paulus. FS für W. G. Kümmel zum 70. Geburtstag*, eds. E. E. Ellis and E. Grässer (Göttingen: Vandenhoeck & Ruprecht, 1975), 196–97.

180. J. Moffatt, *The First Epistle of Paul to the Corinthians*, MNTC, ed. J. Moffatt (London: Hodder & Stoughton Ltd., 1938), 190.

181. G. Delling, s.v. "ἀντιλαμβάνομαι, κ.τ.λ.," *TDNT*, 1:375; Dunn, *Jesus and the Spirit*, 253.

182. Barrett, *1 Corinthians*, 295–96; notice his translation, "gifts of support."

183. Bruce, *1 & 2 Corinthians*, 123; Dunn, *Jesus and the Spirit*, 252.

184. Barrett, *1 Corinthians*, 295–96; see also Dunn, *Jesus and the Spirit*, 253, who follows Barrett's lead, contrary to his earlier position taken on the gifts in Rom 12:6–8. Against this identification, Brockhaus, *Charisma und Amt*, 204.

185. MacGorman, *Gifts of the Spirit*, 55.

186. Thus, the analogy of the body is indeed subordinate to his main paraenetical purpose concerning spiritual gifts. But subordination of purpose does not have to be equated with "polemical purpose"; against B. Daines, "Paul's Usage of the Analogy of the Body of Christ: with special reference to 1 Cor 12," *EvQ* 50 (4, 1978): 72–73.

187. The descriptive designations for vv 14–20 and 21–26 are taken from Dunn, *Jesus and the Spirit*, 264.

188. Brockhaus, *Charisma und Amt*, 172.

189. Dunn, *Jesus and the Spirit*, 265.

190. O. Cullmann, "Oekumenismus im Lichte des biblischen Charisma-

begriffs," *TLZ* 97 (11, 1972): 812.

191. Ibid., 813; see also Käsemann, *Romans*, 339.

192. Against J. Schneider, s.v. "God," *NIDNTT*, 2:79.

193. Priebe, "Charismatic Gifts and Christian Existence," 25.

194. Delling, s.v., "ὑπερβάλλω, κ.τ.λ.," *TDNT*, 8:521.

195. The question of whether Paul composed it independent of and before his first letter to the Corinthians, or specifically for this occasion, is not relevant to the subject under discussion; see Bruce, *1 & 2 Corinthians*, 124; Brockhaus, *Charisma und Amt*, 177–85.

196. Holtz, "Kennzeichen des Geistes," 369.

197. MacGorman, *Gifts of the Spirit*, 58; Dunn, *Jesus and the Spirit*, 271.

198. See Dunn's ch 11, par 57, "The Vision Fades—The Later Pauline Correspondence," in *Jesus and the Spirit*, 345–50. Dale Moody claims to notice the vanishing of the charismatic glow already in Rom 12:6–8, because of the difficulty of defining the gifts cited, *The Word of Truth. A Summary of Christian Doctrine Based on Biblical Revelation* (Grand Rapids: Eerdmans, 1981), 453.

199. H. Windisch, *Der zweite Korintherbrief*, 9th ed., ed. G. Strecker (Göttingen: Vandenhoeck & Ruprecht, 1970), 51; see also R. Bultmann, *Der zweite Brief an die Korinther*, ed. E. Dinkler, KEKNT, ed. F. Hahn (Göttingen: Vandenhoeck & Ruprecht, 1976), 34–35.

200. See A. Plummer, *A Critical and Exegetical Commentary on the Second Epistle of St. Paul to the Corinthians*, ICC, eds. S. R. Driver, A. Plummer, and C. A. Briggs (Edinburgh: T. & T. Clark [repr.], 1966), 21; Bruce, *1 & 2 Corinthians*, 179.

201. So, most commentators; e.g., Lietzmann, *Korinther*, 101; Wendland, *Korinther*, 145; Bultmann, *2 Korinther*, 34; Plummer, *2 Corinthians*, 21; W. de Boor, *Der zweite Brief des Paulus an die Korinther*, WS, eds. F. Rienecker and W. de Boor (Wuppertal: R. Brockhaus Verlag, 1972), 35.

202. C. K. Barrett, *A Commentary on the Second Epistle to the Corinthians*, HNTC, ed. Henry Chadwick (New York: Harper & Row, 1973), p. 67.

203. E.g., RSV: "blessing"; NIV and NEB: "gracious favor"; NASB: "favor."

204. M. Dibelius and H. Conzelmann, *The Pastoral Epistles*, transl. P. Buttolph and A. Yarbro, ed. H. Koester, Hermeneia (Philadelphia: Fortress, 1972); Brockhaus, *Charisma und Amt*; Hasenhüttl, *Charisma*; Dunn, *Jesus and the Spirit*; K. Gábriš, "Charismatische Erscheinungen bei der Erbauung der Gemeinde," *Communio Viatorum* 16 (Summer 1973): 159.

205. E.g., D. Guthrie, *The Pastoral Epistles*, Tyn, ed. R. V. G. Tasker (Grand Rapids: Eerdmans, 1957), 14:11–53; most recently also G. D. Fee, *1 and 2 Timothy, Titus*, GNC, ed. W. W. Gasque (San Francisco: Harper & Row, 1984).

206. Gábriš, "Charismatische Erscheinungen," p. 159.

207. See F. Stagg, *The Book of Acts. The Early Struggle for an Unhindered Gospel* (Nashville: Broadman, 1955), 90–91, for the alternate view, based on the "grammatical antecedent," that the whole group or community laid

hands upon the seven.

208. Piepkorn, "Charisma in the NT," 371; J. N. D. Kelly, *A Commentary on the Pastoral Epistles*, HNTC, ed. H. Chadwick (New York: Harper & Row, 1963), 159; J. D. G. Dunn, *Baptism in the Holy Spirit* (Philadelphia: Westminster, 1970), 167. The reference to the laying on of hands by the presbytery (1 Tim 4:14) and by Paul (2 Tim 1:6) may, in fact, refer to the same event if one considers that the style of 2 Timothy is much more personal than that of 1 Timothy.

209. W. Lock, *A Critical and Exegetical Commentary on the Pastoral Epistles*, ICC, eds. S. R. Driver, A. Plummer, and C. A. Briggs (repr. ed. 1966, Edinburgh: T. & T. Clark, 1924), 54.

210. G. Holtz, *Die Pastoralbriefe*, THKNT, ed. D. E. Fascher (Berlin: Evangelische Verlagsanstalt, 1965), 13:155. Holtz suggests that Timothy needed support and strength. "He may have lacked the self-confidence of the pneumatics and enthusiasts . . . ; hence Timothy may have suffered . . . doubt and depression."

211. P. C. Spicq, *Saint Paul: Les Épîtres Pastorales*, EBib (Paris: J. Gabalda & Co., 1947), 311.

212. See Dibelius, *Pastoral Epistles*, 70; Lock, *Pastoral Epistles*, 53.

213. Hasenhüttl, *Charisma*, 254–55.

3
Charismata as the Church's Equipment for Service

THE CLAIM THAT CHARISMATIC ENDOWMENT equips the church for service is not, first of all, merely a theological construct designed to express something concrete about ecclesiological purposes. Rather, as the exegesis of chapter 2 has demonstrated unequivocally, the view that grace gifts constitute the church's equipment for service arises directly from Paul's usage of the concept of charismata. Service was at the heart of the apostle's concern in almost every reference to giftedness. Perhaps no other statement expresses the identification of gifts (or their bearers) with service as clearly and directly as Eph 4:11–12. Paul declared, "It was he who gave some to be apostles, some to be prophets, some to be evangelists, and some to be pastors and teachers, to prepare God's people for works of service, so that the body of Christ may be built up . . ." (NIV).

Numerous recent scholarly treatments of "charismatic endowment" have emphasized the "service" perspective. Several points of interest emerging from such treatments give rise to questions to be answered in this chapter. One, what are the individual and corporate aspects of charismatic service? Two, in what sense do unity and diversity of grace gifts contribute to the function of service of the latter? Three, is one to understand charismatic gifts for service exclusively in terms of supernaturally bestowed endowment or (also) in terms of natural talents raised to a higher, divine purpose? Four, should spiritual giftedness be regarded as a temporary phenomenon, or was it meant to be permanent, both from the vantage point of church history and from that of a believer's pilgrimage? Albeit fraught with presuppositional biases, these aspects represent legitimate concerns which attempt to capture the meaning and purpose of charismata intended by Paul. This chapter endeavors to interact not merely with the critical material at hand but also with the exegetical basis which was established in the preceding chapter.

INDIVIDUAL AND CORPORATE ASPECTS

The titular statement "Charismata as the Church's Equipment for Service" addresses both the individual and corporate implications of giftedness. Both aspects have been stressed, although sometimes by placing more weight on one at the expense of the other. And those belaboring both aspects seem to appeal to Paul's passages in 1 Cor 12–14, Rom 12:6–8, and Eph 4:7–12 for support of their arguments.

The individual aspect has been emphasized by Käsemann. He maintains that the individual's gift "sets him in a concrete place and equips him for specific service";[1] and with a slightly different nuance, but still to the point, he notes that in the charisma, "the saving will of God comes on the scene as task. . . ."[2] But to affirm with Paul that charismatic endowment is bestowed individually for service does not a priori permit the converse inference that "in Paul's eyes all service in the community is a Spirit-given charisma."[3] Paul's citation of διακονία as a specific gift in Rom 12:7 would suggest the opposite. It may be argued more adequately, however, that every charisma is specifically designed to equip for service, but not every service in the Christian community is necessarily the expression of a bestowed charisma.

Similarly, W. J. Bartling has observed that the relationship of χάρις to χάρισμα sheds light on the purpose of the individual's giftedness. Just as χάρις restores one to "fellowship with God and to a life of community in the new humanity, Christ's body," so χάρισμα sets the same individual a task in that body and empowers him to act.[4] Thus charisma as individuation of God's grace may quite properly be understood as "personalized equipment for service."

When Donald L. Gelpi defines charismata as "service gifts," he probably also reflects on the individual giftedness. But the premise on which he bases this working definition is far removed from the Pauline understanding of charisma as the concretion and personalization of grace. Rather, Gelpi considers "service gifts" as the "normal outcome of growth in the gifts of sanctification." An individual's charisma of service, therefore, ought to be "the specification and concrete personalization of sanctification."[5] Clearly the correlation charismata — service gifts — sanctification rests upon non-Pauline presuppositions, and may point up the mistaken notion of charismatic endowment as a spiritual merit system.

Yet, if the purpose of spiritual giftedness is service, it can be so regarded only insofar as such service is actually perceived by the recipient, or recipients, of the charismatic function(s). The Pauline statement, "but to each one is given the manifestation of the Spirit," was not appended by the prepositional phrase "for the common good" (1 Cor 12:7) in terms of an afterthought. Rather, the latter constituted the qualification for the former claim. Likewise, Paul concluded 1 Cor 12:11 by stressing the individualistic character of the grace gift, namely "he distributes them to each one, just as he determines," only to engage in the major task of demonstrating the necessity for charismatic function in service to the other members of the body (1 Cor 12:12–27). It is "the common life," insists John Howard Schütz, which "is the goal toward which the energies of specific gifts are to be directed. . . ."[6] The intent of individual giftedness for service, therefore, cannot lie in individualism but always points to the higher goal of the corporate body in togetherness.

Considering this, it is not surprising that the corporate aspect of charismatic equipment for service has received much more attention. One can hardly miss Paul's consistent emphasis of corporate service. In fact, all pericopes dealing with charismata were either addressed directly to corporate bodies of believers or they were implicitly pointing to corporateness.

Thomas A. Smail has taken this aspect into account, almost to the point of overemphasis. Yet in the light of contemporary tendencies to individualism in charismatic service, Smail needs to be heard. Stressing the corporate nature of charismatic enablement for service, he maintains, "The gifts of the Spirit are less individual endowments, far less spiritual status symbols, than ways in which we work together within the body of Christ."[7] Charismata, although bestowed upon individuals by the Holy Spirit, are meant for the service unto, and for the upbuilding of, the community as the Spirit directs. Thus, when the gifts of the Spirit function, "they are never at our disposal. There remains something sovereign and elusive about their coming and going."[8] Even from the corporate perspective, it needs to be said again that charismata, as the church's equipment for service, were never meant to be regarded as the property of the church to bask in its charismatic ministry.

Kilian McDonnell has concluded that the primary purpose—and from his argumentation, it would appear, the sole purpose—of charismata can be subsumed under the definition "forms of service to the community." His emphasis of the corporate understanding of charismatic equipment emerges even more clearly when he states:

> The [charismatic] emphasises what is clearly Paul's teaching: the Church is entirely ministerial, made up of members in each of whom the Spirit comes to visibility in a charism or service to others. These charisms . . . are directed outward in service to others. All of them belong to the ordinary life of the normal Christian community, which is charismatically constituted because it is an organism of mutually supporting services directed toward building up the body for mission to the world.[9]

The important point is that the upbuilding of the body of Christ takes on concrete form when the members corporately serve through their God-given functions. In fact, the corporateness of charismatic ministry for the upbuilding of one another, while carried out by individually gifted members, precludes any notion of self-elevation over others. Not only are charismata sovereignly bestowed by the Spirit for the purpose of service, but it would appear from the Pauline perspective that charismata are truly charismata only when they are shared in corporate service. Thus it may be feasible to argue that when Paul listed the gifts in 1 Cor 12:8–10, 28, 29–30, he graded them in terms of their effectiveness for service. According to Banks, "those which make the most profitable contribution to the community's growth are accorded the highest importance."[10]

But as credible as such argumentation may sound, it does not satisfactorily answer the question of serviceability. Apart from the risk of superimposing contemporary schemes of valuation on Paul's lists of charismata, it is difficult to determine which gift makes the most profitable contribution to community growth under varying circumstances and with varying needs. The weakness in Bank's proposal becomes obvious when the list in Rom 12:6–8 is taken into consideration. Nothing in this passage intimates a scale of values according to the profitability of the contributions of the various grace endowments.

Hasenhüttl has taken the foundational notion of individual giftedness for corporate service one step further, suggesting that the deepest expression of ministry toward others is carried out in charismatic representation, or proxy.[11] Taking his cue from the nature of God who reveals himself as the God for others in the church and who always offers and extends his χάρις to others, he applies the principle to the Pauline concept of charismata. Accordingly, in the latter the believer is enabled to witness to and share with his fellow human being the "God for the other"; or, more personally, the "God for you."[12] Hasenhüttl considers the understanding of charismatic endowment for service as the first step toward a necessary deepening of serviceability. In other words, charismatic service for the sake of service tends to succumb to routine. If equipment for service is to be truly charismatic, the endowed must serve out of a concern for relationship with the one, or with those being served.

While the idea of charismatic proxy may not be as explicitly Paul's understanding of how gifted individuals serve one another as Hasenhüttl implies, he nevertheless opens up some profound venues of expressing the individuation of God's grace in charismatic service. The analogy of the human body (1 Cor 12:12–27) includes the concern which one member has for the welfare of all the other members. Thus, Paul conceived of charismatic service essentially as service with a concern for the person(s) intended to receive such service. "One's being for others" is a necessary ingredient of Spirit-prompted charismatic service. Eduard Schweizer has emphasized this correlation in commenting on 1 Cor 12:5, "The gift of grace is always 'service' to the neighbor as the Lord grants it."[13]

At this juncture it needs to be pointed out that charismatic equipment for service embraces both individual and corporate aspects. To pit these aspects against one another is to misunderstand Paul's concept of charismata. Individually bestowed gifts of grace equip individuals for service insofar as these individuals use their charismata to serve the corporate body, even when one particular gift, at a given time, serves only one other member of that body. Individual and corporate service will always lead to, and result in, the upbuilding of the community.

It is in serving others that the charismatically endowed believer will be built up. Hans Freiherr von Campenhausen aptly summarized the individuality and corporateness of spiritual giftedness as follows:

> For Paul it is essential that the sustaining unity of the Spirit, freely given to all, becomes effective in the multiplicity of diverse, individually bestowed gifts. Paul knows of no work of the Spirit in shapeless generality and arbitrary exchange. Rather, one has received this gift, another that gift; thus the church's life is always only manifested in the interaction of diverse spiritual enablings which complement one another and so reveal the fullness and concord of the Spirit of Christ.[14]

UNITY AND DIVERSITY OF CHARISMATA

Von Campenhausen's assessment, cited above, is not only relevant to the issue of individual and corporate aspects of charismatic endowment, it also addresses the perspectives of the unity and diversity of such endowment relative to service. Speaking of unity and diversity of charismata means to evaluate the issue of charismatic equipment for service from another vantage point than that which provided a glance at the individuality and corporateness of giftedness. While the latter was concerned primarily with the believers gifted for service, the former focuses on the source and goal of gifts as well as on the variety of gifts involved in service.

Both the source and the goal of charismata reflect on the aspect of unity. The fact that everyone who has experienced the grace of God has also received some grace gift for service must never detract from the Pauline emphasis on the source of all the charismata; nor from that on the agent of charismata. Thus, the shared experience of grace, which is also the shared experience of the Spirit (1 Cor 12:12), has its unifying factor in God, the source and giver of grace, of the Spirit, and of charismata to be experienced (1 Cor 12:6, 28); and in the Holy Spirit, the agent who bestows charismata sovereignly. Unity of charismata, therefore, is not an accomplishment of a charismatic community; rather, it is the recognition of the foundational provision by the God who gave graciously and without human desert. When the charismatic community acknowledges, in John Koenig's terms, "the Giver behind the gift and utters the words, 'My Lord,' "[15] it recognizes practically that all charismatic endowment for service, for the οἰκοδομή of the body, has its unity in God through the Spirit. Paul's emphasis on the teaching that it was God who arranged the parts of the body as he wanted them (1 Cor 12:18, 24), and its applicatory counterpart with reference to charismatic endowment (namely, that "in the church God has appointed . . ." [1 Cor 12:28]), permits no other conclusion.

Unity finds another expression in the goal of charismatic service. Paul termed it "the common good" (1 Cor 12:7) and "the upbuilding of the church" (1 Cor 14:26, NIV: "strengthening"). The implication seems to be, then, that the shared experience of charismata, although manifested in multiple diversity, fulfills its divine purpose only when the whole community is strengthened. Dunn considers this point indispensable to the claim of being a charismatic community. He writes, "The charismata are always to be seen as service . . . , *as gifts for the body*, given to, or better, *through*, the individual 'for the common good.' . . ."[16]

In fact, one may rephrase the concern for unity by stating that the unity of the charismatically gifted community — that is, the unity which resides in God as the source of grace and in the Spirit — finds its fulfillment only in service resulting in achievement of the divinely purposed goal of the welfare of the whole. Without the οἰκοδομή of the body, the claim for unity remains farcical. Furthermore, any functioning of charismata for purposes other than the upbuilding of the whole community means to fall into the trap of the Corinthian error that Paul sought to correct through 1 Cor 12–14. At its basis, such misuse negates the idea that God is the source of all gifts, and it denies that the individual member has meaning only within the context of the body as a whole—a point which Paul belabored at length, and emphatically, in 1 Cor 12.[17]

If source and goal of charismata depict the aspect of unity plainly, the equally emphasized aspect of diversity of gifts for service lends a certain mystery to the unity of the whole. Diversity of gifts occupied Paul's paraenesis throughout 1 Cor 12–14, as well as in Rom 12:6–8, in order to correct the false sense of spiritual unity perpetrated by the Corinthian monopolizers of ecstatic utterances. Paul's various random listings of charismata reflect diversity *par excellence*. In fact, the unity of the experience of grace is enhanced by the diversity of the grace gifts bestowed and shared in service.

For Paul unity and diversity coincided in the shared experience of the Spirit, for he concluded the list of gifts in 1 Cor 12:8–10 with the profound summary statement, "All these [charismata, manifestations of the Spirit] are the work of one and the same Spirit, and he gives them to each one, just as he wills" (v 11). Diversity of charismata, therefore, does not destroy the unity of the church. The opposite is true; namely, the unity of the church is contingent upon the "proper functioning of the whole range of diverse charismata; without the diversity of the charismata there can be no unity."[18]

Unity and diversity in charismatic endowment for service are complementary, not mutually exclusive, ingredients if the whole community is to be built up by the charismata. It is through the continuous use of these diverse gifts that the unity of the church remains dynamic and centered on the experience of grace. In affirming the need for the diversity of gifts, one acknowledges the individuation of charismata by the Spirit, the interdependence of the diverse gifts with respect to the Giver and with respect to the other gifted members individually and corporately. Nothing could capture the significance of the interplay between the unity and the diversity of charismata in service for the community better than Dunn's concluding statement: "The church as charismatic community means unity in and through diversity—the unity of charis in and through the diversity of charismata."[19]

GRACE ENDOWMENT OR NATURAL TALENT

Few questions concerning charismata, especially when viewed as equipment for service, have stirred as lively a debate as that of whether charismata are grace endowments or natural talents. With the emergence, phenomenal dissemination, and growth of the charismatic movement, the debate has received more attention than ever. The fervor of discussion is not surprising, for two reasons. One, the claims for charismatic endowment in recent years precipitated a natural reaction; a feasible explanation had to be found. Two, the debate may be particularly intense precisely because the question of whether charismata are grace endowments or natural talents is not a Pauline question. Not every answer, therefore, can claim to be the quintessence of Paul's paraenesis. For this reason the debate probably will continue, without finding satisfactory, let alone convincing, answers.

The case for charismata as natural talents generally is not made at the expense of the perspective of sovereignly bestowed concretions of grace. Especially with regard to the gifts of inspired utterance, healing, and miracles, the concession for divine bestowal is granted.[20] Few would insist on the natural order of charismata as radically as René Laurentin has. For him, charismata are supernatural only in terms of being the free gifts of the Spirit. This must not be understood as "superadded to nature," however. "The charism," Laurentin argues, "sets free natural gifts according to the diversity of people and of the human communities."[21] Laurentin's position can hardly be taken seriously from an exegetical point of view, especially since his general purpose is the refutation of the apparent monopolistic attitude concerning charismata on the part of the renewal movement in the Roman Catholic Church.

Karol Gábriš assumes a similar position, at least with regard to the gifts listed in Rom 12:6–8. Concerning their character, he writes, "The charismata of Rom 12 are peculiar because of their natural shape. It is evident then that the nature of charismata must not be sought in their supernaturalness. . . ."[22] Rather, Gábriš sees charismata as the "heightening of the natural." But such a reduction can hardly suffice in the light of Paul's repeated alignment of charismata with God's grace and with the Spirit's sovereign bestowal.

In view of the glaring absence of exegetical support for the equation of charismata with natural talents, scholars have sought to adduce support from the natural order. Arnold Bittlinger, for instance, tends to subsume the supernatural elements of charismata under the natural realm.

He claims, "On the one hand they are natural abilities and capacities which are innate in us, and on the other hand it is the Holy Spirit who is quickening and enlarging these capacities."[23] Bittlinger's assertion does not rest on the Pauline passages dealing with charismata. Instead, he uses the analogy of an apple tree to make his point. The seed which ultimately produces the apple tree originally lies dormant in the dry ground until rain saturates the ground and causes the seed to sprout. Out of this emerges the eventual apple tree whose fruit is to nourish and refresh others. In the analogy, the rain causing the change in the seed is likened to the Holy Spirit who "brings forth" charismata in our lives, corresponding to our originality.[24] But as logical as such argumentation may be, it is fraught with the weakness of speculative hypothesizing to answer logically what remained mysteriously unanswered by the Apostle Paul.

Georg Eichholz has warned against the simplistic equation of charismata with natural talents. Charismata do not correspond to the model of talents in which

> the distribution of talents has the nature of a privilege, and the talented person always has something uniquely his own through which he can excel. In his field, he is efficient while the other is merely a dabbler.[25]

But then he draws the astute contrast with what he considers to be the Pauline perspective, "Charismata are always the result of the creative wealth and goodness of the Spirit."[26]

This contrasting statement of Eichholz places the emphasis on the grace character of charismata. The exegetical evidence supporting the case for the gracious bestowal of gifts by the Spirit is strong enough for some scholars to conclude that no other perspective is possible. MacGorman maintains, on the basis of 1 Cor 12:4, that "charismatic endowment is not a do-it-yourself kit. Only the Holy Spirit can give these gifts."[27]

From the same premise, Dunn comments, "These manifestations of the Spirit are marked out for Paul as given (not achieved by man), as expressions of divine energy (not human potential or talent), as acts of service which promote the common good (not for personal edification or aggrandizement)."[28] In fact, for Paul, every charisma could only be supernatural because it was God-given and Spirit-bestowed. Thus a charisma used for service for the good of all can properly be called a charisma only when it is exercised in *"unconditional dependence on and openness to God."*[29]

But does this mean that God does not, by his Spirit, avail himself of human abilities at all when charismata are being exercised in service? In answering this question, the focus shifts to the various mediating attempts which decline a position at either extreme. Typically, instead of an "either-or" stance, theirs is one of "both-and." Even Dunn—perhaps the outstanding contemporary champion of the cause for charismata as grace endowment only—concedes that charisma may "chime in with an individual disposition and temperament, and will certainly make use of natural abilities (even glossolalia makes use of the vocal chords)."[30] However, his concession cannot be considered a compromise in terms of mixing the human and the divine in the character of charismata.

Banks, after noting correctly that the placement of charismata between the two poles is not a distinction Paul would have made, leaves the door open for a connection of charismata with natural talents. These, he argues, are also "implanted by the prior creative activity of God, or by social advantages conferred by the circumstances of life."[31]

Moltmann affirms, on the one hand, that the one Spirit gives charismata to every individual. Each receives his "specific share and calling, which is exactly cut out for him, in the process of the new creation." Hence, charismata are not to be equated with natural abilities. On the other hand, he asserts, "In principle every human potentiality and capacity can become charismatic through a person's call, if only they are used in Christ."[32] For Moltmann, therefore, the key issue is not what the believer has potentially or supernaturally given to him by the Spirit; rather, the determining factor, that which renders grace gifts charismatic, is their modality. In other words, "It is not the gift itself that is important, but its use."[33]

Käsemann does not hesitate to combine grace endowment and natural talent; for since the boundaries of charismata are ἐν κυρίῳ, and since the church is not a "neutralized zone," sheltered from the profane world, everything can become charisma to the believer. He suggests, "A thing can only be purely secular to the man who thinks of it in this way. As nothing is charisma in itself, so nothing is secular in itself." This venue can only lead to the conclusion which Käsemann does reach; namely, "All things stand within the charismatic possibility and are holy to the extent to which the holy ones of God make use of them."[34]

It is not surprising, therefore, that Käsemann becomes an outspoken proponent of the divine-human synthesis in his more recent commentary on Romans. Here he specifies, "The aptitudes and gifts present in the individual, insofar as they are taken into the service of Christ and developed as functions of community life against religious individualism, may be described without reserve as charismata."[35]

Jean-René Bouchet, with particular application to the charisma of the discernment of Spirits, supports the Käsemannian synthesis. For him, the term "spiritual gift" does not necessarily mean that God gives someone a specific gift without regard to his natural gifts. Concerning the gift of discernment, Bouchet says that this charisma makes

> use of such acquired qualities as the ability to listen, intuition, delicacy and psychology. It brings a pinch of humor to them. In fact, every gift is cultivated to the extent that the receiver is converted to Christ, has had the Gospel preached to him, is well educated and at peace with himself.[36]

But Bouchet's rather idealistic notion tends to create an elitist church comprised of experts in their individual fields, in whom the charismata are invested. Charismatic function, then, becomes gathered up in the clergy, a point Bouchet seems to support. However logical such views may appear, they betray an underlying conflict with Paul's insistence that charismata are given to everyone in the community of faith, as God wills.

Perhaps the distinction "natural talents" is unfortunate; it implies that the natural talents are of lesser value than the supernatural grace endowments. The issue is one of consciousness of God's grace in the believer's and, consequently, in the community's life. Disliking the descriptions of natural versus supernatural, Koenig suggests that "the awareness of grace transforms what believers receive into gifts *from God*, whether they be 'natural' or 'supernatural' according to the philosophical and scientific standards of the day."[37]

If natural abilities are likewise God's gifts to mankind, and these are surrendered to God in the experience of his grace, is he not sovereignly able to bestow those talents again as charismata upon the one who surrendered them to God? The source would always be God. Indeed, it is the origin which is, and remains, constitutive of the charismata. This, Hasenhüttl maintains, differentiates grace gifts from talents. Talent remains "talent" and retains its meaning even when it is severed from its giver. The grace gift, however, when loosed from its source, "turns into pagan manticism or into common 'traits.' "[38]

Ultimately, however, the issue must remain unresolved. Paul did explicitly affirm the grace character of charismatic endowment, but remained silent on the question of natural talents or abilities. Yet, it would be foolhardy not to leave the door open to allow God to be magnanimous enough to bestow a surrendered talent in the form of a charisma on the one who submits in obedience to his control (cf. Rom 12:1–2).

PERMANENCE OR TEMPORARINESS OF CHARISMATA

The debate over the permanence or temporariness of charismata has ranged along two lines of argument. One, it is claimed, primarily by some scholars outside the classical pentecostal and charismatic movements, that certain charismata were never meant to be permanent but, instead, proved to be temporary and ceased after the first few centuries of the church. Two, charismata as equipment for service are said to be given as the believer's permanent possession and not temporarily, as some assert. In the case of the latter, charismata are given to a believer only for a specific ministry at a specific point in time and in a specific place.

The first argument is generally not advanced on the basis of thorough exegesis, but receives its impetus from presuppositional and historical biases. Scriptural evidence is brought to bear more in terms of prooftexting than in terms of contextual interpretation. The second line of argument deserves a closer look since it seeks to understand the Pauline concept of charismatic service for the church's upbuilding.

The case for the historical temporariness of grace gifts is generally made under the assumption that the more spectacular charismata, in particular the so-called sign gifts, were given especially for the authentication of the first-century apostolic message of Christ. At any rate, these gifts were for the era prior to the completion of the canon of Scripture. The demonstration of these gifts—which include miracles, healing, tongues, interpretation, and discernment[39]—was no longer necessary and, consequently, was replaced by the written record of God's revelation in the canonized Scriptures.

In support of this argument, proponents usually point to 1 Cor 13:8–9 where Paul maintained the temporariness of prophecies and tongues. But the weakness of the argument is self-evident. First, Paul cited as temporary not only prophecies and tongues, but also the gift of knowledge. Therefore, if tongues and prophecy were representative of the miraculous sign gifts, by implication it follows that knowledge was representative of all the other charismata. It is poor exegesis to pick and choose parts of the text for that which supports one's presuppositions, without regard for grammatical units and for context. Second, it is significant that of all the relevant passages dealing with charismata, only

1 Cor 13:8 speaks of prophecy in the plural, προφητεῖαι. Paul may, therefore, not have made reference to the charisma of prophetic utterance per se, but simply to the manifold prophecies in the course of the church's ministry. Third, when Paul said, "when perfection comes, the imperfect disappears" (13:10), he did not refer to the end of the apostolic era[40] or to the completion of the canon of Scripture.[41] Instead, following most interpreters and, in the context of the entire chapter more plausibly, Paul focused on the eschatological revelation of Christ at the end of this present age. All charismata, Paul said in essence, will cease at that time.

Nothing in the text of 1 Cor 13, or in any other Pauline passage concerned with charismatic endowment, permits the conclusion that certain gifts of the Spirit were to function for a limited initial period only. For Paul, all Spirit-bestowed charismata were given for the upbuilding of the body. There exists no reasonable exegetical warrant for denying that the same gifts which equipped the church for service then should fulfill the same purpose today. Bank's assessment is pungent at this point: "As far as their duration is concerned, they are clearly not temporary in character but permanent features of the community life as long as this present age lasts."[42] It is this writer's view that, given the virtual nonexistence of exegetical support to the contrary, the argument for the temporariness of charismata should be laid *ad acta*. The distinction is imposed upon the text, and exposes a foundational problem; namely, that one's religious experience (or nonexperience) seeks to conform the text to itself rather than to be open towards the Word, submitting one's religious experience (or nonexperience) to the text.

The second line of argument for the temporary or permanent character of charismata seeks to apply exegetical findings from the Pauline corpus with regard to an individual's giftedness. Viewed from the perspective of temporary charismatic endowment, Ronald P. Brown defines grace gifts as "the manifestations of the power of the Spirit of God for the ministry to which that person is called at that particular time."[43] Accordingly, charismata are not "closely defined entities or permanent abilities, but possible ways in which the Spirit may choose to work at a particular time in a particular individual."[44]

It could be reasoned that the singular descriptions λόγος σοφίας and λόγος γνώσεως (1 Cor 12:8) denote singular utterances at a given time and place. Likewise, Baker maintains, the plural forms of the charismata in 1 Cor 12:9–10 indicate multiple occurrences of these gifts at a particular time.[45] The fact that the Spirit is the subject in v 11 means that he bestows these gifts upon individuals in the community of faith wherever and whenever he chooses to do so. In essence, this could be construed to mean that one individual possibly may have bestowed upon him, by the Spirit, several different grace gifts during his lifetime as a Christian.

More difficult to comprehend—and, therefore, less feasible exegetically—is the listing of both singular and plural forms of the charismata in favor of temporariness. Next to 1 Cor 12:11, perhaps the strongest indicator of the temporary nature of charismata, is Paul's encouragement to the Corinthians to seek earnestly after gifts which they did not exercise at that time (1 Cor 12:31a). For Banks, this is also the only sensible conclusion of the interpretation of 1 Cor 14:1.[46]

On the other hand, Schürmann pleads for the permanent character of giftedness by appealing to Paul's analogy of the human body. An individual member does not change his particular function(s) within the body as long as the member belongs to the body. Charismata, he maintains, build an orderly structure which, in turn, reflects permanence, not fickle temporariness.[47] The unity of the body resides in the strength of the permanence of the latter. As further support of the permanence of charismatic endowment, one might add the charisma of apostleship which was given to Paul (although he never identified it as such). Throughout his ministry he claimed to be an apostle of Jesus Christ, as the introductory verses of all of his letters (except Philemon) suggest. But if Paul is cited as evidence for the gifts' permanence, the experience of his gifts also points to their temporariness. For example, only in a few instances is Paul said to have exercised the charismata of healing (e.g., Acts 14:8–10; 19:11–12; 28:8–9. 2 Tim 4:20 also points to the nonpermanence of the gift of healing in Paul; for he writes, "Trophimus I left sick at Miletus.") and of miraculous deeds (e.g., Acts 16:16–30; 28:1–6); nor does he himself claim to have had these gifts either permanently or temporarily. The textual evidence suggests the latter.

The argument by Schürmann appears to be solid, if the body analogy alone is used for comparison. But in the light of the broader context, as well as from the vantage point of Paul's experience, Schürmann may have unreasonably restricted the body metaphor to the aspect of permanence; that is, to the unity of the body. It is doubtful that Paul had only this idea in mind when writing 1 Cor 12:12–27. It may be more appropriate to expect both temporariness and permanence in harmonious interplay, both in the Pauline churches and on the contemporary church scene.

SUMMARY

The claim that one of the primary purposes for charismatic endowment is to equip the believer for service is readily accepted on exegetical grounds. Contention does not revolve around this general assertion, however; rather, when the focus shifts from this central affirmation of the Pauline perspective of charismata to any one of the particular issues dealt with in this chapter, opinions differ widely. There is the tendency to render exclusive specific concerns which ought to yield to the greater concern of giftedness for the sake of service. Paul did not place in juxtaposition the individual and corporate aspect, nor the unity and diversity of charismata. The issue of whether grace endowment or natural talent describes more appropriately what constitutes a charisma is not a Pauline issue and will, therefore, always elicit but fragmentary and temporary answers.

Likewise, the question of the temporariness or permanence of charismata in the church necessarily remains hypothetical since Paul did not directly address it. There is no textual precedent for the acceptance of the view that charismata, in part, gave way to the canon of Scripture.

Rather than viewing each element in isolation, it may be more Pauline to gather all elements into one focus, thereby affirming what Paul did assert unequivocally: that charismata served the upbuilding of the whole body. Emphasis of various details at the expense of a holistic approach unnecessarily fragments the Pauline concept of charismata.

If it is legitimate to regard the purpose of charismatic giftedness as the equipment for service, would it not also be proper to address the subject from the perspective of ministerial function? It is to that view that the next chapter will give attention.

NOTES

1. Käsemann, *Romans*, 335.
2. Ibid., 316.
3. Ibid., 340.
4. Bartling, "Congregation of Christ," 69.
5. D. L. Gelpi, *Charism and Sacrament: A Theology of Christian Conversion* (New York: Paulist, 1976), 63–64.
6. J. H. Schütz, "Charisma and social reality in primitive Christianity," *JR* 54 (1, 1974): 60. Similarly, S. Fowler, "The Continuance of the Charismata," *EvQ* 45 (7, 1972): 172. He points out that Paul viewed charismatically gifted individuals always as members of the body, whose gifts were to be used for service within the context of, and to, the body.

7. T. A. Smail, *Reflected Glory: The Spirit of Christ and Christians* (Grand Rapids: Eerdmans, 1975), 131.

8. Ibid., 124.

9. K. McDonnell, "The Experience of the Holy Spirit in the Catholic Charismatic Renewal," in *Conflicts About the Holy Spirit*, eds. H. Küng and J. Moltmann, in the series *Concilium: Religion in the Seventies* (New York: Seabury, 1979), 128:99–100. But McDonnell probably understands the corporate purpose of charismatic service too inclusively in his listing of examples, lumping prophet, teacher, labor organizer, healer, librarian, sweeper of floors all together as charismatic endowment. How does a twentieth-century labor organizer, or a librarian, contribute to the upbuilding of a specific body of believers and, thus, serve the whole?

10. Banks, *Paul's Idea of Community*, 98–99. Similarly, K. McDonnell, *Charismatic Renewal and the Churches* (New York: Seabury, 1976), 6. Against the application of serviceability as scale of value, see J. A. Baker, "A Theological Look at the Charismatic Movement," *Churchman* 86 (Winter 1972): 262.

11. Hasenhüttl, *Charisma*, 238–42. See also Koenig, *Charismata*, 108–10, for a similar emphasis.

12. Hasenhüttl, *Charisma*, 239.

13. E. Schweizer, *The Holy Spirit*, transl. R. H. and I. Fuller (Philadelphia: Fortress, 1980), 94.

14. H. Freiherr von Campenhausen, *Kirchliches Amt und geistliche Vollmacht in den ersten drei Jahrhunderten*, BHT, ed. G. Ebeling (Tübingen: J. C. B. Mohr [Paul Siebeck], 1953), 14:61.

15. Koenig, *Charismata*, 127.

16. Dunn, *Jesus and the Spirit*, 264. Italics are his.

17. G. Eichholz, *Die Theologie des Paulus im Umriss* (Neukirchen-Vluyn: Neukirchener Verlag, 1972), 277.

18. Dunn, *Jesus and the Spirit*, 265.

19. Ibid.

20. Implicitly in Hollenweger, "Creator Spiritus," 33.

21. R. Laurentin, "Charisms; Terminological Precision," in *Charisms in the Church*, eds. C. Duquoc and C. Floristan, in the series *Concilium: Religion in the Seventies* (New York: Seabury, 1978), 7–8.

22. Gábriš, "Charismatische Erscheinungen," 156.

23. A. Bittlinger, "The Charismatic Worship Service . . . ," *Studia Liturgica* 9 (1973): 222. See also his definition of charismata in *Gifts and Graces*, 72, and the more elaborate treatment of the issue in ch 2 of *Gifts and Ministries*, intro. K. McDonnell, transl. C. K. Dyck (Grand Rapids: Eerdmans, 1973), 15–20.

24. Bittlinger, "The Charismatic Worship Service," 222.

25. Eichholz, *Die Theologie des Paulus im Umriss*, 277.

26. Ibid.

27. MacGorman, *Romans, 1 Corinthians*, 137–38; similarly, in *The Gifts of the Spirit*, 28–29, where he notes that charismata are "handed down by the Spirit of God; they are not worked up by men."

28. Dunn, *NIDNTT*, 3:702–3; *Jesus and the Spirit*, 255. See also Doughty,

"Priority of χάρις," 178; M. Griffiths, *Grace-Gifts: Developing What God Has Given the Church* (Grand Rapids: Eerdmans, 1978), 14; Culpepper, *Evaluating the Charismatic Movement*, 81, 87.

29. Dunn, *Jesus and the Spirit*, 256, (italics his).

30. Ibid., 255. See also Oudersluys, "Purpose of Spiritual Gifts," 219, who qualifies similarly, "While a spiritual gift is not simply another name for a natural talent . . . a spiritual gift can be exercised through a natural talent."

31. Banks, *Paul's Idea of Community*, 100.

32. Moltmann, *The Church in the Power of the Spirit*, 295–97.

33. Ibid., 297.

34. Käsemann, "Ministry and Community," 72. Schweizer argues similarly in "What is the Holy Spirit?" xiii.

35. Käsemann, *Romans*, 334. Cf. Conzelmann, *TDNT*, 9:404–5.

36. J-R. Bouchet, "The Discernment of Spirits," transl. D. Livingstone, in *Conflicts About the Holy Spirit*, eds. H. Küng and J. Moltmann, in the series *Concilium: Religion in the Seventies* (New York: Seabury, 1979), 128:104.

37. Koenig, *Charismata*, 58–59; italics his. Hollenweger reaches the same conclusion by noting that for Paul charisma was a term that designated both the supernatural, extraordinary, and the more natural, ordinary (e.g., to be married or to be single), "Creator Spiritus," 33.

38. Hasenhüttl, *Charisma*, 114–15.

39. See J. F. Waalvoord, "Contemporary Issues in the Doctrine of the Holy Spirit: IV, Spiritual Gifts Today," *BS* 130 (10, 1973): 315–28.

40. E.g., Fraikin, "Charismes et ministères," 462. he argues that when Paul submitted the charismata to the criterion of the upbuilding of the body, he already legitimated a church at a time when these charismata would have ceased to play an essential role; namely, approximately at the end of the first century AD. However, on the evidence for the continuity of charismatic endowment through the patristic era, see Jacques Serr, "Les charismes dans la vie de l'église; temoignages patristiques," *Foi et Vie* 72 (1973): 33–42; E. A. Stephanou, "Charismata in the Early Church Fathers," *The Greek Orthodox Theological Review* 21 (1976): 125–46; J. Laporte, "The Holy Spirit, Source of Life and Activity According to the Early Church," in *Perspectives on Charismatic Renewal*, ed. E. D. O'Connor (Notre Dame: University of Notre Dame Press, 1975), 57–99.

41. E.g., Waalvoord, "Spiritual Gifts Today," 319–20; see Culpepper, *Evaluating the Charismatic Movement*, 83–85, for an excellent rebuttal of this line of argument. Consult also Smail's treatment of the issue in *Reflected Glory*, 38–39.

42. Banks, *Paul's Idea of Community*, 95. Culpepper concludes, "If those gifts served to edify the body then, what basis do we have for thinking they could not bring edification in our day?" *Evaluating the Charismatic Movement*, 85.

43. Brown, "Gifts of the Holy Spirit," 176.

44. Baker, "Interpretation of 1 Cor 12–14," 232.

45. Ibid.

46. Banks, *Paul's Idea of Community*, 93.

47. Schürmann, "Die geistlichen Gnadengaben," 248.

4

Charismata as Ministerial Function

THE EQUATION OF CHARISMATA with ministerial function is not a vestige of a church moored in historical tradition; nor is it a reaction to the phenomenon of contemporary charismatic decentralization of ministry. Rather, as Schulz has remarked astutely, "the problem of relationship between charisma and office is as old as the New Testament."[1] In this chapter, "ministerial function" is understood primarily, but not exclusively, as clerical office, following the argumentation of a host of interpreters of Paul's concept of charismata.

In the following, therefore, the purpose of charismata needs to be examined again, in order to respond to the assertion that charismatic gifts are equivalent to ministerial functions or offices. Some interpreters of Paul have served notice that charismata are to be understood as evangelistic or missionary functions in a pagan environment. The claim needs to be tested by the Pauline criteria governing charismata. The road is then paved for an evaluation of the notion that charismata are directed just as much toward the world as toward the community of believers. It remains to be seen whether these contemporary claims are valid when they are weighed in the balance of an exegesis of the Pauline materials.

When the question is raised whether charismatic endowment as ministerial function is to be understood in terms of the corporate body or in terms of ministerial office, the answers which recent critical literature provides tend to diverge greatly. The claims in favor of ministerial office are often based on appeals to tradition and to the need for continuity of ecclesiastical order.[2] Consequently, the call for a dissemination of ministry to the whole body by charismatic communities also tends to be perceived as a challenge, if not as a threat, to the clergy of traditional church structures.[3]

EQUATION OF CHARISMATA WITH OFFICES

The argument for equating grace gifts with ministerial offices, according to some interpreters, receives its biblical support from Paul's instruction in 1 Cor 12:28 and Eph 4:11. Paramount to the claim for scriptural precedence, of course, are the references to charisma in the Pastoral Letters (1 Tim 4:14, 2 Tim 1:6). "Charisma," concludes Dunn, "has become power of office" in the Pastorals.[4]

But while the idea of the equation of charisma with office may receive conditional support from the Pastorals, Käsemann detects a certain shift from charisma to office already in Rom 12:6–8. In the gifts mentioned in that passage he sees "archetypes of later ecclesiastical institutions."[5] At first glance, Käsemann's statement may appear to be a correction of his earlier view expressed in his article, "Ministry and Community in the New Testament." In the latter he maintains that the relationship between church and office is determined exclusively by the perspective of charisma. Consequently, "a situation in which all Christians are regarded as endowed with charisma is a situation which does not admit the possibility of . . . the right of representative action in the cultus . . . [namely of] persons thought of as specially privileged. . . ."[6] In this manner Käsemann negates the "prerogative of official proclamation, vested in some specially commissioned individual. . . ." Rather, every charismatic believer is "an office-bearer of Christ."[7]

Yet, the gathering up of the charismatic believer and the office bearer under the category of ministry is not to be understood strictly in terms of democratic leadership, for, Käsemann argues, this line of reasoning could be turned around to mean that no one is actually an office bearer. Paul seemed to recognize different levels of charismatic ministry.

On the other hand, Käsemann readily recognizes that the Pauline communities also knew of ministries which would be defined as clerical offices today. This recognition emerges clearly from the statement that "universal obligation does not imply the equality of all."[8] Thus it is important to ask Käsemann how Paul's understanding of ministry could, at the same time, be charismatic and official. In an attempt to grasp Käsemann's "both-and" approach, Brockhaus has suggested that the former did not subscribe to the antithetical tension between charisma and office which is held, among others, by von Campenhausen and Schweizer. Instead, Käsemann chose to place charisma and ministerial office in a dialectical tension in which both are united in the concrete exercise of office; that is, in the actual ministry.[9]

To hold charisma and office in dialectical tension may prove to be more feasible from the exegetical perspective than is commonly presumed. Since Paul's teaching on charismata was the projection of the doctrine of justification into his ecclesiology, as Käsemann has emphasized repeatedly, the basis of all charismatic ministry rests on the χάρις of God. Thus, Paul never claimed that his ministry (or office), e.g., his apostleship, derived from a charisma. But he asserted frequently that his ministry derived from God's grace (e.g. Rom 12:3; Eph 3:7).[10]

Further, the dialectical tension is also noticeable in the Pauline metaphor of the human body. He recognized that some members carry out more visible—and, therefore, more prominent—functions than others. Nevertheless, those enjoying prominence are always only members conjoined with those whose functions, precisely because they are less noticeable, deserve greater honor (1 Cor 12:21–26). Applied to the charisma as ministerial function, this means that it is to be fully expected that certain charismatic functions, such as those specifically numbered in 1 Cor 12:28, are carried out with greater frequency and with greater prominence than other functions. The latter may be less noticed but they are equally important to the unity and upbuilding of the body. Moltmann probably has the same dialectical relationship in focus when he suggests that while the whole community is commissioned (unity) to function charismatically and ministerially, not everyone in the community has the same task (diversity).[11]

The tension between charisma and office has also surfaced in the Roman Catholic scholarly community. Rahner recognizes, on the one hand, the charismatic element which transcends the institutional order, but he cannot divorce himself, on the other hand, from the notion that the church acts as the administrator of the gifts of the Spirit. For him, "it is not possible to conceive of the official Church and hierarchy as the institutional organizer and administrator of the gifts of the Spirit in the Church, unless one sees it from the start as being itself: the law-giving Church, first and foremost the Church of the charismata."[12]

While Rahner's presentation pays little attention to the Pauline concept of charismatic ministry, Heribert Mühlen endeavors to do justice to the diversity and multiplicity of charismatic functions within the church. But it appears that he accepts the Pauline perspective only for charismata exercised outside the structured liturgical setting. The gifts functioning in the worship of the community are exercised only by the *one priest* who presides over the meeting. Charismata are for the purpose of the upbuilding of the body, but only in terms of worship.[13] Mühlen does not clarify how he justifies the clerical monopoly on some charismata, especially in the light of 1 Cor 12:7, 11, 28–30. Clearly, Mühlen allows institutional tradition to determine exegesis. Whereas Paul would have argued that because there is charisma there is ministry, Mühlen's argument would have to be reversed to say that because there is a ministerial office there is charisma.

In contrast to Rahner and Mühlen, McDonnell does not institutionalize charisma when he speaks of the latter as ministry. Rather, charismata are "operations or manifestations of the Holy Spirit in and for the Christian community." Through them the Holy Spirit "comes to visibility in the church in service functions."[14] To this point, McDonnell follows the Pauline delineation; for different kinds of gifts are also different kinds of service given for the common good (1 Cor 12:5–7).

However, McDonnell seems to yield to the institutional perspective of giftedness when he places charismata in a hierarchy according to the degree of serviceability. If Paul cited apostles, prophets, and teachers, in that order, as first, second, and third (1 Cor 12:28), as God's gifts to the body, it does not necessarily follow that they are at the top of the hierarchy because they fulfill more immediately a service or ministry to others.[15] Although McDonnell does not make the correlation explicitly, by implication his suggested hierarchy of service functions smacks of the institutionalization of charismata.

It needs to be emphasized again that Paul's listing of certain gifts in 1 Cor 12:28–30 was first of all the direct result and application of the preceding pericope concerning the functioning of the human body. Second, the order in the listing was almost certainly related to the Corinthian situation. In their enthusiastic but disorderly use of inspired speech in the gathered community, the Corinthian glossolalists had spurned the orderliness of the apostolic, prophetic, and didactic ministry.[16] The order of the grace endowments listed in 1 Cor 12:28 should, therefore, be regarded situationally and not as a normative hierarchy of ecclesiastical offices.

In radical departure from the traditional Catholic understanding of charismata, Hans Küng declares boldly, "The Pauline charisma cannot be subsumed under the clerical office, but the clerical offices can be subsumed under the charisma."[17] And Hasenhüttl envisions a church characterized by charismatic ministry as follows: "When the church is understood as existence for one another, that is when every believer, every charismatic has his concrete, equally valuable task for the upbuilding of the whole church, then her origin in the Spirit will be recognized more clearly in the community's practice and her basic charismatic structure will be realized in life's everyday experiences."[18]

Such an understanding of charismata can only be the fruit of a study of the Pauline concept of charismata, which takes seriously the apostolic paraenesis. The relationship between charisma and ministry can no longer be interpreted along the traditional movement from commission to appointment or recognition to charisma. Paul's perspective on that relationship requires a reversal of movement from charisma to recognition to commission.[19]

But the radical reaction to the equation of charisma with ministerial function or office by placing them in antithesis does not constitute the final verdict.[20] Perhaps it is to assert too much to claim Pauline precedent for either position. Indeed, Bartling has established correctly that I Cor 12 is not designed to answer the question of *how* the gifts are related to specific church offices.[21] Paul did affirm, however, that charisma and ministerial function always belong together in the church. Since charismata are given to all believers in the community of faith, all believers will necessarily also function in some expression of ministry. There is no incontrovertible evidence that Paul even entertained the notion that charismatic ministry would be shifting from the entire community to a select few who held ministerial offices.

CHARISMATA AS MINISTRY IN EVANGELISM AND MISSIONS

The conception of grace gifts as ministerial functions has spawned the perspective that charismata actually have a much farther-reaching purpose than simply the upbuilding of the body or the equipping of believers for ministry to the body. Evangelism and crosscultural communication of the gospel in missionary outreach have been suggested as vehicles through which charismata reach beyond the boundaries of the local church body into the world. The claim deserves examination for two reasons.

One, appeal is often made to the Pauline concept of charismata for support. According to Hollenweger, the boundaries of the πρὸς τὸ συμφέρον and of the οἰκοδομὴ τῆς ἐκκλησίας have been drawn too narrowly by interpreters of Paul. "The common good," reasons Hollenweger, "reaches beyond our own narrow confines and conceptions of church-related experience."[22] Paul's view of "the common good" must be inclusive of the charismatic ministry in evangelism and missions[23] in the world. The reference to the gift of evangelism, carried out by τοὺς εὐαγγελιστάς (Eph 4:11), may also be adduced in support. The primary purpose of evangelism is the proclamation of God's redeeming grace in Jesus Christ. Its direction, therefore, is toward the world outside the community of believers. Only indirectly is the οἰκοδομή of the church also achieved, namely through accepting into the church those who respond affirmatively to the function of the charisma of evangelism. The issue in Eph 4:11 was not at all the establishment of the evangelist as a ministerial office. Congruent with all of the charismata in the Pauline perspective, the gift of evangelism, whether used intraculturally or crossculturally, was also bestowed distributively upon individuals in the church.

One might interpret 1 Cor 14:24–25 in terms of an example of prophetic utterance with an evangelistic thrust. Prophecy, in that case, becomes the equivalent of evangelism, at least functionally, and constitutes the vehicle of the message of salvation with resultant conviction and confession. But the context hardly permits the idea of an evangelistic charisma of prophecy. The presence of pagans in the gathered community of believers is at best incidental to Paul's overall concern in 1 Cor 14. The response of ἰδιῶται was first of all a consequence of Christians sharing the Word of God with one another, not directly with the outsider."[24]

Two, the charge is increasingly leveled against the traditional interpretation that the latter does not take into account the viability of non-Western Christian perspectives of charismata. When charismatic evangelism functions on a crosscultural level, the modality of the response and the implementation of Paul's concept of charismatic community may indeed vary from those traditionally expected and experienced in the Western church world. Hollenweger has called for a reappraisal of what is commonly accepted as charismatic in the Christian community. The problem is perhaps not so much that the charismatic experience in Third-World Christian groups might not be identifiable as Pauline in essence. Instead, the problem may, at least in part, lie in Western cultural presuppositions by which the "Third Church's"[25] exercise of charismatic function is gauged. At stake may not be their nonconformity to the criterion of the Pauline concept of charismata but their necessary acceptance on the part of the Western church.

Hollenweger chides the restriction of charismata to individual believers and to religious experiences. Such restrictions, he maintains, are unknown to Paul and to many Third-World Pentecostals.[26] He notes that for Third Church communities, charismata are often understood in terms of "demonstrations, political analysis, land reform, organizing agricultural and production co-operatives without foreign capital and experts." In other words, charismata enable believers to become truly human.[27]

Clearly, for the traditional interpretation of Paul's concept of grace gifts, the drift reflected in Hollenweger's appeal is too far to the left to qualify as Pauline. But Hollenweger's concerns must not be dismissed too hastily. He must be heard at the point of the charge that Western interpreters of Paul tend to forget that they, too, confine their understanding of charismatic function to culturally conditioned modalities. Could it not be that the charismatic modalities of the Third Church, as noted above, also serve the upbuilding of the body of Christ within their cultural milieu? Paul's radical correction of the Corinthian πνευματικά may very well reflect a similar shock treatment which, in turn, may have contributed to the reluctant acceptance of Paul's authority on the part of the Corinthians.

CHARISMATA FOR THE WORLD

The foregoing arguments inevitably lead to the question of whether Paul conceived of charismata both as grace endowments to believers in the community and as special gifts operative in the world. With this context in mind, Ellis defines charismata as "those gifts of the eschatological age that *create* and *empower* the Christian community."[28] If charismatic ministry is needed to create the Christian community, it may be valid to say that charismata are also directed to the world. The ultimate result would remain the same in the οἰκοδομή of the church.

The function of charismata toward the world may also be demonstrated in the miracle of Pentecost when τὰ μεγαλεῖα τοῦ θεοῦ were proclaimed in ἡμετέραις γλώσσαις, a multiple expression of simultaneous charismata.[29] Schweizer also points out that "the gifts of the Spirit which erupt in the community and serve each member merge surprisingly in Rom. 12:14–15 into the gifts which cross boundaries between church and world."[30] Another parallel may be drawn between the function of the Spirit and that of the gifts which the Spirit bestows. According to Jn 16:7–10, the function of the Spirit is directed worldward for the purpose of convicting it "of guilt in regards to sin and righteousness and judgment." At the same time the Spirit dwells in the believer, attests to his sonship (Rom 8:9–17), and endows him with enabling graces for ministry (1 Cor 12:7, 11). Since the Spirit has this dual function, it is reasonable to presume that the charismata he bestows follow the same pattern of dual function. They are given to the members of the body of Christ for service to the body and to the world.

Admittedly, the point is argued on the grounds of inference and implication. Unfortunately, Paul did not make a single explicit statement concerning the worldward function of the gifts of the Spirit, let alone a statement of affirmation of such function. And an exegesis of the Pauline materials does not provide a definitive answer. Yet, in the light of the arguments discussed, the function of charismata to the world and in the world cannot be ruled out categorically.

SUMMARY

For Paul, the relationship between charisma and ministry was always integral. Charisma without ministry denies the purpose of charismatic endowment and ignores its grace character. Ministry without charisma denies the dynamic which makes ministry effective and ignores its gift character.

Two aspects need to be maintained with regard to charisma and ministry. One, charismata are given to believers in the context of the community. In Paul's view, every congregation was a charismatic community, "a body shaped and informed by the Spirit of Christ and his gifts."[31] Two, all charismata are bestowed for the purpose of ministry. In fact, it follows from Eph 4:11 that the charismata are the enabling graces which equip the saints to minister to the whole body of Christ.[32]

But the affirmation of charisma as ministerial function does not legitimate either the equation of charisma with office or the placing in antithesis of charisma and office. To opt for either position means to go beyond the information given in the Pauline letters. Perhaps it is safest to hold charisma and office in dialectical tension, ministry being their common function and purpose. Schürmann summarized the issue well: "The differentiation of charismatic and non-charismatic ministries is untenable for Paul; even the more official ministries must be viewed charismatically."[33]

When charismata are understood as ministerial functions in evangelism and missions, the exegetical foundation becomes decidedly thinner. The arguments, pro and con, seem to be predicated more upon presuppositional and cultural notions. A viable exegesis of the Pauline concept of charismata which reflects the radically different perspective of the Third Church has yet to appear. And without it, consensus, as well as mutual acceptance, will continue to rest on speculation. Perhaps it would ease the tension to a degree if one did not belabor the point of a different interpretation of Paul by the churches of the Third World. Instead, it might be more appropriate to speak of a radically different application of the principles which emerge from Paul's view of charismata, in the light of differing cultural conditions.

Charismatic ministry in and to the body of Christ represents an indispensable Pauline fact. But that is not true of the notion that charismata are equally directed worldward—at least not from an exegetical standpoint and not with the same clarity. The work of the Spirit in and to the world belong to John's special insights (e.g., Jn 16:8–11). Nevertheless, Paul's understanding of charismatic function opens up the possibility that certain charismata, particularly that of evangelism, are designed for ministry to the world. The relationship between the Holy Spirit and the gifts he bestows seems to demand the concession that both relate to the community of believers and to the world. Ultimately, however, all charismata serve the upbuilding of the body, either directly or indirectly.

The rather lively debate on the subject of charismata understood as ministerial functions or offices may well receive continued impetus in the wake of the rapid expansion of the charismatic movement around the world. Whether new ground will be tilled to provide a better perspective on the interpretation of Paul's concept of grace gifts remains an open agenda.

In recent years this debate has further spawned the notion that the charismata which constitute ministerial functions also reflect something about the relationship of charismata and authority. Could authority be a viable expression of charismata? It is this question on which the following, and last, chapter will focus.

NOTES

1. Schulz, "Die Charismenlehre des Paulus," 448.

2. For instance, J. E. Agrimson, "The Congregation and the Gifts," in *Gifts of the Spirit and the Body of Christ: Perspectives on the Charismatic Movement*, ed. J. E. Agrimson (Minneapolis: Augsburg, 1974), 111, asserts that "charismatic gifts have their best meaning in the continuity of the tradition (doctrine, liturgy, and history)."

3. J. Baker observes this keenly in "A Theological Look at the Charismatic Movement," 271. He notes, "Those liable to feel most threatened . . . are the clergy, especially those who think 'the special ministry' is virtually their sole prerogative." See also Ferdinand Hahn, "Charisma und Amt: die Diskussion

über das kirchliche Amt im Lichte der neutestamentlichen Charismenlehre,"
ZTK 76 (1979): 419–49. Hahn correctly calls for a different orientation since
democratization can hardly be Paul's choice of order. Even such attempts as
"christocracy" or "pneumatocracy" are misnomers since charismata as gifts
from God can never be regarded as forms of κρατεῖν, 447.

    4. Cf., Dunn, *Jesus and the Spirit*, 348; Käsemann, "Ministry and
Community," 128. With reference to the Pastorals, Conzelmann also speaks of
the "charisma of office," *TDNT*, 9:406.

    5. Käsemann, *Romans*, 34.

    6. Käsemann, "Ministry and Community," 78.

    7. Ibid., 81.

    8. Ibid., 82.

    9. Brockhaus, *Charisma und Amt*, 41. See his treatment in pt 1 of his
work, "Frühchristliches Amt und Charismen in der theologischen Diskussion."
Although Brockhaus recognizes the Käsemannian dialectic, he includes him in
ch 1 in which he discusses seminal scholars who plead for the antithesis between
charisma and office.

    10. See Banks, *Paul's Idea of Community*, 99.

    11. Moltmann, *The Church in the Power of the Spirit*, 308.

    12. Rahner, *The Spirit in the Church*, 52. Perhaps one has to regard
Rahner's reference to the "papal charisma of infallibility" from the same ecclesiastical perspective. However, the Pauline paraenesis has nothing to say, even
remotely, about such a charisma. Rather, it seems to be a "gift," bestowed upon
one individual, by the Roman Catholic Church. See also Hasenhüttl's able
evaluation in pt 5, "Die Wiederbesinnung auf die Charismatische Struktur der
Gemeinde," in *Charisma*, 321–35, esp. 343–53.

    13. H. Mühlen, "The Charismatic Renewal as Experience," in *The Holy
Spirit and Power*, ed. K. McDonnell (Garden City, NY: Doubleday & Co.,
1975), 112. For a less ecclesiastical and more closely Pauline perspective, see
Mühlen's more recent attempt at a charismatic theology, especially chs 5–7, *A
Charismatic Theology: Initiation in the Spirit*, transl. E. Quinn and T. Linton
(New York: Paulist, 1978), 126–208.

    14. McDonnell, *Charismatic Renewal and the Churches*, 6.

    15. Hahn defines these as "kerygmatic charismata"; they enjoy priority
status since Paul also accorded them preference. While the other "gifts in the
Christian community enrich its life and ministry without being indispensable,"
the kerygmatic gifts (apostle, prophet, teacher) remain "constitutive for the
existence of the Church," "Charisma und Amt," 437–38.

    16. See Käsemann's discussion in "Ministry and Community," 78–84.
S. Fowler, "Continuance of the Charismata," 176, makes the same point when
he writes, "While it is possible so to exalt the office that the charismata are left
no room, it is also possible so to exalt the charismata as to reduce the office to a
meaningless name, a mere formality. This was the Corinthian danger." See also
Hahn, "Charisma und Amt," 437–38.

    17. H. Küng, *Die Kirche* (Freiburg im Breisgau: Herder KG, 1967), 225,
ET, *The Church*, Image Books (Garden City, NY: Doubleday & Co., 1976),
245; Schulz, "Die Charismenlehre des Paulus," 448–54.

18. Hasenhüttl, *Charisma*, 359.

19. Moltmann, *The Church in the Power of the Spirit*, 311. See Moltmann's cogent insights into the subject in "The Charge to the Community and the Assignments within the Community," 300–14, in which he attempts to interpret charismatically the tasks of the community; hence from within the church, not hierarchically.

20. Most recently R. Y. K. Fung has called for a reexamination of the subject in "Charismatic vs. Organized Ministry: An Examination of an Alleged Antithesis," *EvQ* 52 (Oct 1980): 195–214.

21. Bartling, "Congregation of Christ," 74.

22. Hollenweger, "Creator Spiritus," 38.

23. See Culpepper, *Evaluating the Charismatic Movement*, 87.

24. Banks, *Paul's Idea of Community*, 93.

25. Hollenweger notes, in "Creator Spiritus," 35, that the term, relating to the church in the Third World, is taken from W. Bühlmann, *The Coming of the Third Church. An Analysis of the Present and Future of the Church* (Slough, England: St. Paul Publications, 1976).

26. That Paul does admit to the presence of πνευματικά outside the church is quite evident from 1 Cor 12:2, 3. But it is equally evident that he acknowledged as χαρίσματα only the manifestations of the Spirit, and only as far as these were subjected to the christological test of 12:3 as well as to the criterion of οἰκοδομή. See ch 2.

27. Hollenweger, "Creator Spiritus," 38.

28. Ellis, "Christ and Spirit in 1 Corinthians," 272. Italics are this writer's.

29. See Acts 2:5–13. The ἡμετέραις γλώσσαις of v 11 may be identical to the γένη γλωσσῶν of 1 Cor 12:10. But in the light of Acts 2:8, the statement ἀκούομεν ἕκαστος τῇ ἰδίᾳ διαλέκτῳ ἡμῶν, the charisma of tongues should, in this instance, be understood as the charisma of languages. The gift of tongues in 1 Cor 12–14 requires the attendant gift of interpretation, while the tongues which functioned in Acts 2:5–13 were perfectly intelligible. See Koenig, *Charismata*, 82–84, and Griffiths, *Grace-Gifts*, 66. Griffiths contends that most Pauline references to charismata actually are relevant only in terms of missionary service. Tongues, then, become the ability to learn new languages, and the gift of interpretation refers to the translation from a foreign language into that spoken in a certain place.

30. Schweizer, *The Holy Spirit*, 130.

31. Bartling, "Congregation of Christ," 77.

32. Oudersluys, "The Purpose of Spiritual Gifts," 214.

33. Schürmann, "Die geistlichen Gnadengaben," 246.

5
Charismata as Expression of Authority

THE ISSUE OF AUTHORITY in the ecclesiastical context has been traditionally linked with the debate on apostolic authority or with that on
recognized ministers or office bearers in the church. While the subject
was moot for a long time, in recent years the discussion of authority has
become the center of attention. Several factors may have influenced and
contributed to this development.

One, the popularization of the notion of charisma—or perhaps more
accurately, the contemporary misuse of the Pauline concept of charismata
—has played a major part in this development. The significance of the
conventional usage of "charisma" lies in its association with "authority."
Hence, popularly, charisma has been defined as "a particular personal
magnetism or spiritual quality that enables the possessor to exert influence
over broad masses of people and elicit their support."[1] The implication
of manipulation is too obvious to be ignored. In particular, the comparison with the Corinthian use (or misuse) of certain charismata points out
the ramifications of espousing the popular perspective on charisma.

Two, reference has already been made to Max Weber's sociological
approach to charisma[2] which, in turn, gave rise to the popular understanding described above. Weber did not link charisma directly with
authority. Rather, in a peculiar twist of the Pauline emphasis of the gifts
themselves, he stressed the charismatic person whom he described as an
ideal type, a natural leader. Charisma, then, is first of all associated with
leadership which has its authentication in unique qualities or charismata.
But once Weber established the correlation between the "charismatic"
person and "leadership," it was but a short step to include perhaps
inevitably, the correlate "authority." In Weber's functional definition, a
charismatic "seizes the task for which he is destined and demands that
others obey and follow him by virtue of his mission."[3] Clearly, authority
lies at the very heart of Weber's concept; charisma and authority are

personified in the charismatic leader. Whether it is appropriate and valid to draw a straight line from this conception to the Pauline paraenesis concerning charismata remains to be evaluated exegetically.

Three, the investigation of the character of apostolic authority has received significant attention in recent studies. In particular, the recent monograph of John Howard Schütz[4] exemplifies the renewed concern with understanding better Paul's position on authority and its implications for the contemporary church scene. It is significant that Schütz devotes an entire chapter to the question of how charisma and authority might be related.[5]

Four, to a large extent it has been the renewed critical study of Paul's concept of charismata which has brought into sharper focus the relationship of authority to charismatic giftedness.[6] Further, and directly responsible for an intensified study, the universal burgeoning of the charismatic movement has contributed to the interest in the subject. Charismatically gifted persons who lack adequate teaching on the relationship of charismata to authority tend to usurp the former in order to express—and thereby misuse—authority.[7]

It is not the purpose of this chapter to provide an in-depth examination of authority from the pertinent Pauline materials. But the attempted equation of charismata with authority, both in its secular and religious expressions, and in its critical scholarly presentations, demands an answer from the Pauline interpretation of charismata. That answer will be sought by evaluating the following factors: one, the basis for the claim that charismata and authority are synonymous terms; two, the scope of charismata and authority in the church; and three, the manipulative tendencies of charismatic authority.

THE EQUATION OF CHARISMA AND AUTHORITY—ITS BASIS

Three approaches have been suggested relative to ascertaining the basis of charismata as expression of authority. One, as Schütz has sought to establish in his monograph, as well as in a concurrent article,[8] charismata and authority clearly are correlative ideas. Central to his claim is the Weberian notion of charismatic leadership which Schütz then proceeds to link with Paul's understanding of charismata. Granted, Schütz deals primarily with apostolic authority. But that is precisely what allows him the association of charismatic leadership with apostolic authority.

How does Schütz turn from apostolic authority to charismata as basis for the former, especially when he readily—and correctly—admits that Paul never explicitly tied his role as apostle to the idea of charisma? For one thing, he does not draw sharp distinctions between χάρις and χάρισμα as a basis for apostolic activity. The former may render the apostle "indistinguishable from any other Christian," in which case the notion of special status on account of authority would be virtually eliminated. The latter may become a credible basis when Paul's own ministry and gifts are considered as an example of what the apostle regarded as charismatic.[9] But that basis would be possible only if it could be shown that Paul considered his charismata as of a different piece of cloth from those of the communities he established and addressed in his correspondence.

For another, Schütz applies Weber's sociological categories to Paul's concept of charismata. Therefore, Schütz argues, "The idea of *charismata* as a first-century sociological category for the expression of authority depends on our seeing the spiritual gifts as a power phenomenon, and authority as the interpretation of power."[10] And elsewhere he states, more specifically, "Ascription of charisma is really the ascription of authority, the manifestation of charisma a manifestation of authority.[11]

This line of argument may be valid strictly from the observation of the Corinthian understanding of charismata as power or authority, but certainly not from the Pauline perspective. If apostolic authority coincided with one or more charismata in 1 Cor 12–14, it might be found in the apostolic correction of the Corinthian error. Explicitly and exegetically, however, it cannot be maintained that Paul considered charismata as expressive of authority; nor that bestowal of certain gifts meant ascription of special authority.

Two, it has been suggested that charisma and authority in the community are subsumed under and based upon the bearers of office. This is particularly true, Gábriš suggests, in the Pauline conception of authority, which is the authority or power of the Spirit. Authority, therefore, is associated with persons, not with things or abstract concepts.[12] In fact, O. Betz defines ἐξουσία as "the power to act . . . by virtue of the position he holds."[13] The term describes "the power which decides."[14] In both definitions the emphasis is on the person who has authority. Perhaps Paul's substantial description of charismata in terms of the bearers of these gifts (apostles, prophets, teachers, 1 Cor 12:28) could be construed as implicit ascription of authority. But the apostle's effortless interchange of terminology, both in Rom 12:6–8 (nouns and participles) and in 1 Cor 12 (nouns for gifts and nouns for the charismatically endowed) does not lend itself to the singling out of office bearers as bearers of authority. At least Paul did not make that distinction. For him, none of the charismata were particularly authority-oriented. It seems to be part of the significance of the Pauline metaphor of the body that charismatic functioning of the community of faith meant the equalization of concern and respect for the differing exercises of gifts. Authority was not eliminated thereby, but its focus shifted from the few to the whole.

Three, it was undoubtedly the undue stress on the authority of the "few," namely of the office bearers, in whom the church traditionally recognized the merging of charismata and authority, that compelled von Campenhausen to maintain a categorical disjuncture between the two concepts. In his own words, "The most conspicuous characteristic of the Pauline view of the community is . . . the fundamental elimination of all formal authority within the individual community. . . ."[15] As radical as von Campenhausen's argument may appear to be, he does not throw out all authority from the congregation. But he denies the claim for "formal" or "official" authority on the basis of the Pauline concept.

Thus von Campenhausen's position seems to be congruent with that of Käsemann. For the latter, Paul accorded authority only to the servant and then only in the concrete fulfillment of his ministry in the church.[16] But in making such a statement, the equation of charisma and authority is clearly negated. There exists no exegetical basis for it. On the other hand, Käsemann's modification already points to the next issue to be evaluated.

THE SCOPE OF CHARISMATA AND AUTHORITY IN THE CHURCH

Just as charismata are first of all given to individual believers in the community and for the community, so authority has meaning only within the context of the community. It is in this sense that Käsemann sees the relationship between authority and charisma in the community.[17] To assert that authority and charisma belong together is quite different from the previous claim that the two ideas are synonymous, so that the one becomes the other. Instead, it may be more appropriate to speak here of the scope (and hence also of the boundary) of charismata and authority. According to Käsemann, their scope and boundary are in the church. Therefore, "as charisma is only manifested as genuine in the act of ministry, so only he who ministers can have authority and that only in the actual exercise of his ministry."[18] In this case, service represents the functional scope of authority and the latter is clearly secondary to the former.

It has already been pointed out that charismata and authority properly belong in the context of the church. Thus, the locus must also be regarded as expression of scope. While Paul seemed to consider himself, in his authority, as independent from all people (Gal 1:1), he did not regard that authority as a superior, for the community untouchable, privilege. Instead, even as apostle, Paul stood within the charismatic community, and his authority was always exercised within the church. For this reason Paul was able to assure the Corinthians, "Not that we lord it over your faith, but we work with you for your joy" (2 Cor 1:24, NIV).[19] It is this writer's contention that in 1 Cor 12:28 Paul may have placed the apostles first to underscore that as apostle and charismatically endowed individual, he submitted his authority to the boundary and context of the community. Thus, just as he shared in the charismatic giftedness of the Corinthians, so he considered his authority in the community to be shared authority with that of the Corinthians.

Two additional reference points deserve mention in this connection. One, probably Paul's two most central concerns for the proper functioning of charismatic ministry in the community were the συμφέρον and the οἰκοδομή. The first was to keep the charismatic from self-aggrandizement while the second pointed the charismatic ministry to its highest function, the upbuilding of the community. If charismata and authority belong together in the context of the church, συμφέρον and οἰκοδομή are equally applicable to authority.[20]

Two, Paul fully expected the Corinthians to exercise their authority in the community as well. In evaluating and testing what other members may have been uttering prophetically, he encouraged the other prophets, if not the entire congregation, to "weigh carefully what is said" (1 Cor 14:29). Indeed, the exhortation to "test everything" (1 Thes 5:21) was also addressed to the whole community. And, as Dunn reminds us, "Not least in importance is the community's responsibility to recognize and acknowledge the manifest charismatic authority of those who do not spare themselves in the service of the church. . . ."[21] The harmonious and orderly functioning of a charismatic community is possible only when charismata and authority are shared in the community. Only then are the scope and boundary of both taken seriously.

THE MANIPULATIVE TENDENCIES OF
CHARISMATIC AUTHORITY

Probably the gravest danger of regarding charismata as expression of authority is the proclivity to misuse both. The Corinthian situation, as Paul reflected it in 1 Cor 12–14, provides ample indication of this. The Corinthian enthusiasts manipulated the community by misusing the charisma of glossolalia. Thereby they set themselves up as superior to the rest; hence, as authority. It was this *malaise* which Paul addressed and sought to correct. What the Corinthians considered as spiritual authority, expressed in glossolalia, was actually anarchy and threatened the Corinthians' self-understanding as community. It is safe to say that the charismatic authority of the individual believer receives (and maintains) its significance only in submission to the charismatic authority of the entire community.[22] To the extent that this act of submission is being exercised, both charismata and authority find their mutual fulfillment in the service of others, without becoming manipulative.

SUMMARY

These cursory deliberations on the question of whether charismata are expressive of authority should suffice to affirm unequivocally that, from an exegetical stance, the equation is not valid. At every turn in Paul's treatment of the Corinthian situation, there are indicators of the fact that the recent attempt to equate charismata with authority has more affinity with the Corinthian misunderstanding of both concepts than with the corrective Pauline paraenesis.

But it is fully in keeping with Paul's handling of his own apostolic authority, and with its relation to the charismatically endowed community, to maintain that in the church charismata and authority belong together. Both are legitimated in service which takes seriously the συμφέρον and the οἰκοδομή of the whole community. Clearly, there is no room for authoritarianism or manipulation where charismata and authority are submitted to the community. Perhaps the real issue is not whether charismatic endowment is an expression of authority. Instead, the ultimate test of the validity of the equation may be found in the christological test in 1 Cor 12:3.

NOTES

1. Piepkorn, "Charisma in the New Testament," 369.
2. See ch 1 for bibliography.
3. M. Weber, *Economy and Society: An Outline of Interpretive Sociology*, eds. G. Roth and C. Wittich, transl. E. Fischoff et al. (New York: Bedminster Press, 1968), 3:1112; see also Schütz, "Charisma and Social Reality," 62.
4. J. H. Schütz, *Paul and the Anatomy of Apostolic Authority*, NTSMS, vol. 26, ed. M. Black (Cambridge: Cambridge University Press, 1975).
5. Ibid., 249–80.
6. See Dunn, *Jesus and the Spirit*, especially 271–300; Hasenhüttl, *Charisma* 77ff; A. Satake, "Apostolat und Gnade bei Paulus," *NTS* 15 (1968–69): 96–107; A. Lemaire, "Ministries in the New Testament; recent research," transl. from French, *BTB* 3 (6, 1973): 133–76.
7. This is particularly evident in the frequently used introductory formula to a prophetic utterance, "Thus says the Lord, . . ." and in the usage of the first person sg. pron. "I" to convey God's word to a congregation (e.g., "Thus says the Lord, behold I will bless you . . ."). Both are preferred prophetic terminology because they lend weight to what is being said and because they render message and messenger authoritative.
8. Schütz, "Charisma and Social Reality in Primitive Christianity."
9. Schütz, *Paul and Apostolic Authority*, 251.
10. Ibid., 252; italics are his.
11. Schütz, "Charisma and Social Reality," 52. Schütz makes the interesting point that a discussion of authority should include not only the notion of leadership but also the correlative idea of "following the leader." This, he suggests, "raises the interesting question of whether one of the charismatic gifts might be that of following." The ramifications are significant, particularly when "following" is incumbent upon all believers as well. The situation would then be similar to that of διακονία which is every believer's task and yet, for Paul, also was a specific grace gift (Rom 12:7, 1 Cor 12:5).
12. Gábriš, "Charismatische Erscheinungen bei der Erbauung der Gemeinde," 159.
13. O. Betz, "Authority," *NIDNTT*, 2:601.
14. W. Foerster, "ἐξουσία, κ.τ.λ.," *TDNT*, 2:566.
15. von Campenhausen, *Kirchliches Amt und Geistliche Vollmacht*, 75–76.
16. Käsemann, "Ministry and Community," 78; cf. Schulz, "Die Charismenlehre des Paulus," 449.
17. Ibid., 78.
18. Ibid., 78.
19. See also 2 Cor 2:10, 10:6. Likewise, the exercise of Paul's authority in 1 Cor 5:1–5 is typical of the self-limitation of his authority. He considers the locus of his authority to be the community.
20. Foerster, *TDNT*, 2:570.
21. Dunn, *Jesus and the Spirit*, 292.
22. See Banks, *Paul's Idea of Community*, 186.

Conclusions

IT IS TIME NOW TO MAKE SOME CONCLUDING observations. The concern was to investigate first of all Paul's concept of charismata; not theologically as it has been done most frequently, but exegetically. The study of the term's etymology and particularly the study of its usage in secular and religious literature led to the only feasible conclusion: that the concept of charismata is uniquely Pauline. Paul gave the term its distinctiveness. Of all the terms Paul employed to convey the idea of "gift," "charisma" was his preferred term because it expressed best the concrete outworking of God's grace in believers in the church. The concept embraced every facet of life, personal lifestyle and experience, as well as corporate redemption and service. Paul seemed to conceive of Christian existence as charismatic existence.

But even more characteristically, Paul regarded all the communities of believers as charismatic communities. He did not give the slightest indication that he knew of charismatic and noncharismatic churches. That distinction is a post-Pauline invention and is dubious, at best.

Whether Paul employed the term "charismata" to express giftedness or the peculiarly Corinthian designation "spiritual gifts," or simply "spirituals," he used both synonymously. It is the Holy Spirit who bestows the gifts of grace; conversely, where God's grace has been received by faith, the Spirit dwells and dynamically lets grace become concrete in diverse charismata. In Paul's attempt to redirect the Corinthians' mistaken notion that πνευματικά express a certain spiritual superiority, he posits χαρίσματα as the apostolic corrective.

On the basis of the exegesis of the Pauline pericopes, the following affirmations emerge as the apostle's seminal understanding of grace gifts: One, charismata are expressive of the diversity of gifts bestowed by the sovereign Spirit upon the members of the body of Christ. Thus, charismatic gifts are concretions and individuations of the grace of God. Two, every Christian is a member of the body of Christ and, hence, charismatic. Three, charismata are given for service, not for self-gratification. The highest functional purpose of giftedness is the upbuilding of the body in love. All gifts, whether directly or indirectly, must ultimately contribute toward the οἰκοδομή of the whole community of faith. Four, none of the gifts of grace is worthless; and none is worth less than any other. John V. Taylor has expressed it well, "All the Spirit's gifts are wonderful; all are marked by a certain spontaneity; but none is meant to be weird. They are incalculable, not incomprehensible."* Five, charismata are not to be understood hierarchically; otherwise their grace character is no longer paramount. Yet, in terms of function, some gifts may be more visible, more regularly exercised, and thus more prominent. Six, while both charismata and authority are operative in the church, charismata themselves never express authority. Finally, all expressions of ministry are to be understood charismatically.

So far the emphasis has been on the insights gained from the exegetical investigation. But the study was also concerned with the evaluation of and interaction with recent critical literature on the subject of charismata. For the most part, the exegetical and theological sources consulted indicate hopeful signs that Paul's understanding of charismatic endowment and ministry is being taken more seriously than in the past. Of course, widely different hermeneutical procedures and divergent presuppositions necessarily lead writers to different conclusions.

Denominational concerns often determine, or at least influence, the critical study of charismata and the conclusions reached. This is true of writers within the charismatic movement, as well as of those from the noncharismatic tradition. One cannot but hope for the day when denominational priorities will also be humbly submitted to the more important task of exegesis. It is not denominational affiliation which must inform exegesis. Instead, in the first place, the latter must inform denominational concerns.

The observation is rather painful that the most pertinent contributions to a better comprehension of Paul's concept of charismata come from outside the pentecostal/charismatic tradition. Could it be that this lack of critical study on the part of the latter is directly related to their experiential orientation? If so, it may also reflect a tacit admission that experience alone is an unreliable and insufficient hermeneutical principle. Experience must be submitted to the test of exegesis.

---

*John V. Taylor, *The Go-Between God: The Holy Spirit and Christian Mission* (Philadelphia: Fortress Press, 1973), 202.

Conversely, if objective study remains only that, however insightful and pertinent it may be, it misses the dynamic and experience of charismatic ministry. Balance will come about only when experience and exegesis interact in the body of Christ. And only then does the christological criterion of charismata take on its fullest meaning, ". . . no one can say 'Jesus is Lord,' except by the Holy Spirit" (1 Cor 12:3).

Selected Bibliography

Agrimson, J. Elmo. "The Congregation and the Gifts." In *Gifts of the Spirit and the Body of Christ: Perspectives*, ed. J. Elmo Agrimson. Minneapolis: Augsburg, 1974.

Allo, P. E.-B. *Saint Paul: Première Épître aux Corinthiens*, 2nd ed. In Études Bibliques. Paris: J. Gabalda & Co., 1956.

Baker, David L. "Interpretation of 1 Corinthians 12–14." *Evangelical Quarterly* 46 (10, 1974): 224–34.

Baker, John P. "A Theological Look at the Charismatic Movement." *Churchman* 86 (Winter 1972): 259–77.

Banks, Robert. *Paul's Idea of Community: The Early House Churches in Their Historical Setting*. Grand Rapids: Eerdmans, 1980.

Barrett, Charles Kingsley. *A Commentary on the Epistle to the Romans*. In Harper's New Testament Commentaries, ed. Henry Chadwick. New York: Harper & Row, 1957.

———. *A Commentary on the First Epistle to the Corinthians*. In Harper's New Testament Commentaries, ed. Henry Chadwick. New York: Harper & Row, 1968.

———. *A Commentary on the Second Epistle to the Corinthians*. In Harper's New Testament Commentaries, ed. Henry Chadwick. New York: Harper & Row, 1973.

Bartling, W. J. "Congregation of Christ, a Charismatic Body; an Exegetical Study of 1 Corinthians 12." *Concordia Theological Monthly* 40 (2, 1969): 67–80.

Bauer, Walter. *A Greek-English Lexicon of the New Testament and Other Early Christian Literature*, 2nd ed. Transl., rev. and augmented by William F. Arndt, F. Wilbur Gingrich, and Frederick W. Danker. Chicago: University of Chicago Press, 1979.

Baur, Ferdinand Christian. *Paul the Apostle of Jesus Christ, His Life and Work, His Epistles and His Doctrine. A Contribution to the Critical History of Primitive Christianity*, vol. 2, 2nd ed.; edited after the author's death by Eduard Zeller. Transl. A. Menzies. London: Williams & Norgate, 1875.

Bittlinger, Arnold. "Charismatic Renewal: An Opportunity for the Church," transl. *The Ecumenical Review* 31 (7, 1979): 247–51.

———. "The Charismatic Worship Service in the New Testament and Today." *Studia Liturgica* 9 (1973): 215–29.

———. *Gifts and Graces: A Commentary on 1 Corinthians 12–14*. Transl.

Herbert Klassen. Grand Rapids: Eerdmans, 1967.

———. *Gifts and Ministries*. Introduction by Kilian McDonnell. Transl. Clara K. Dyck. Grand Rapids: Eerdmans, 1973.

Black, Matthew. *Romans*. In the New Century Bible (New Testament), ed. Matthew Black. London: Marshall, Morgan & Scott, 1973.

Bouchet, Jean-René. "The Discernment of Spirits." Transl. Dinah Livingstone. In *Conflicts About the Holy Spirit*, eds. Hans Küng and Jürgen Moltmann. In the series Concilium: Religion in the Seventies, Vol. 128. New York: Seabury Press, 1979.

Brandt, Robert L. *Spiritual Gifts*, Christian Service series, No. 15. Brussels: International Correspondence Institute, 1980.

Bridge, Donald, and David Phypers. *Spiritual Gifts and the Church*. Downers Grove, Ill.: Inter Varsity Press, 1973.

Brockhaus, Ulrich. *Charisma und Amt: Die Paulinische Charismenlehre auf dem Hintergrund der frühchristlichen Gemeindefunktionen*, 2nd ed. Wuppertal: Theologischer Verlag Rolf Brockhaus, 1972.

Brown, Colin, ed. *The New International Dictionary of New Testament Theology*, 3 vols. Grand Rapids: Zondervan, 1975–1978.

Brown, Ronald P. "Gifts of the Holy Spirit." *Reformed Review* 28 (Spring 1975): 171–82.

Bruce, Frederick Fyvie. *The Epistle of Paul to the Romans*. In The Tyndale New Testament Commentaries, Vol. 6, ed. R. V. G. Tasker. Grand Rapids: Eerdmans, 1978.

———. *1 and 2 Corinthians*. In the New Century Bible (New Testament), ed. Matthew Black. Grand Rapids: Eerdmans, 1971.

Bultmann, Rudolf. *Der zweite Brief an die Korinther*, special ed. Ed. Erich Dinkler. In Kritisch-Exegetischer Kommentar über das Neue Testament, begründet von H. A. W. Meyer, ed. Ferdinand Hahn. Göttingen: Vandenhoeck & Ruprecht, 1976.

———. *Theology of the New Testament*, 2 vols. Transl. Kendrick Grobel. New York: Charles Scribner's Sons, 1951/1955.

Conzelmann, Hans. *1 Corinthians*. Transl. James W. Leitch. Bibliography and references by James W. Dunkly. In Hermeneia: A Critical and Historical Commentary on the Bible, ed. George W. MacRae. Philadelphia: Fortress, 1975.

Corley, Bruce. "Jews, the Future, and God." *Southwestern Journal of Theology* 19 (Fall 1976): 42–56.

Cranfield, C. E. B. *A Critical and Exegetical Commentary on the Epistle to the Romans*, 2 vols., 6th rewritten ed. In the International Critical Commentary, ed. J. A. Emerton and C. E. B. Cranfield: Edinburgh: T. & T. Clark, 1975.

Cullmann, Oscar. "La prière selon les épîtres pauliniennes: conférence donnée à l'Université d'Athène le 11 Mai 1978." *Theologische Zeitschrift* 35 (3–4, 1979): 90–101.

———. "Oekumenismus im Lichte des biblischen Charismabegriffs." *Theologische Literaturzeitung* 97 (11, 1972): 809–818.

Culpepper, Robert H. *Evaluating the Charismatic Movement: A Theological and Biblical Appraisal*. Valley Forge: Judson Press, 1977.

Daines, Brian. "Paul's Use of the Analogy of the Body of Christ, with Special Reference to 1 Corinthians 12." *The Evangelical Quarterly* 50 (4, 1978): 71–78.

Dautzenberg, Gerhard. *Urchristliche Prophetie: Ihre Forschung, ihre Voraussetzungen im Judentum und ihre Struktur im ersten Korintherbrief.* In Beiträge zur Wissenschaft vom Alten und Neuen Testament, 6th ed., Vol. 4. Eds. Siegfried Herrmann and Karl Heinrich Rengstorf. Stuttgart: Verlag W. Kohlhammer, 1975.

―――. "Zum religionsgeschichtlichen Hintergrund der διάκρισις πνευμάτων (1 Kor. 12:10)." *Biblische Zeitschrift* 15 (1, 1971): 93–104.

De Boor, Werner. *Der zweite Brief des Paulus an die Korinther.* In Wuppertaler Studienbibel, ed. Fritz Rienecker and Werner de Boor. Wuppertal: R. Brockhaus Verlag, 1972.

De LaPotterie, Ignace. "Χάρις paulinienne et χάρις johannique." In *Jesus und Paulus.* Eds. E. Earle Ellis and Erich Grässer. Göttingen: Vandenhoeck & Ruprecht, 1975.

Denney, James. *St. Paul's Epistle to the Romans*, Vol. 2. In The Expositor's Greek Testament, ed. W. Robertson Nicholl. Grand Rapids: Eerdmans, 1956.

Dibelius, Martin and Hans Conzelmann. *The Pastoral Epistles.* Transl. Philip Buttolph and Adela Yarbro. In Hermeneia: A Critical and Historical Commentary on the Bible, ed. Helmut Koester. Philadelphia: Fortress, 1972.

Dodd, C. H. *The Epistle of Paul to the Romans.* In The Moffatt New Testament Commentary, ed. James Moffatt. New York: Harper & Brothers, 1932.

Doughty, D. J. "The Priority of χάρις. An Investigation of the Theological Language of Paul." *New Testament Studies* 19 (1972–73): 163–80.

Dunn, James D. G. *Baptism in the Holy Spirit.* Philadelphia: Westminster, 1970.

―――. *Jesus and the Spirit: A Study of the Religious and Charismatic Experience of Jesus and the First Christians as Reflected in the New Testament.* Philadelphia: Westminster, 1975.

―――. "A Note on δωρεά." *Expository Times* 81 (8, 1970): 349–51.

―――. "Prophetic 'I'-Sayings and the Jesus Tradition: The Importance of Testing Prophetic Utterances Within Early Christianity." *New Testament Studies* 24 (1, 1978): 175–98.

Eichholz, Georg. *Die Theologie des Paulus im Umriss.* Neukirchen-Vluyn: Neukirchener Verlag, 1972.

Ellis, E. Earle. "Christ and Spirit in 1 Corinthians." In *Christ and Spirit in the New Testament*, eds. Barnabas Lindars and Stephen S. Smalley. Cambridge: Cambridge University Press, 1973.

―――. "'Spiritual' Gifts in the Pauline Community." *New Testament Studies* 20 (1, 1974): 128–44.

Evangéline, Sister. "The Monastic Life: a Charismatic Life in the Church." *The Ecumenical Review* 31 (7, 1979): 273–78.

Fee, Gordon D. *1 and 2 Timothy, Titus.* In Good News Commentary, ed. W. Ward Gasque. San Francisco: Harper & Row, 1984.

Findlay, G. G. *St. Paul's First Epistle to the Corinthians.* In The Expositor's Greek Testament, Vol. 2; ed. W. Robertson Nicholl. Grand Rapids: Eerdmans, n.d.

Fowler, Stuart. "The Continuance of the Charismata." *Evangelical Quarterly* 45 (7, 1973): 172–83.

Fraikin, Daniel. "'Charismes et ministères' à la lumière de 1 Cor. 12–14." *Église et Théologie* 9 (10, 1978): 455–63.

Fung, Ronald Y. K. "Charismatic vs. Organized Ministry: An Examination of an Alleged Antithesis." *Evangelical Quarterly* 52 (10, 1980): 195–214.

Gábriš, Karol. "Charismatische Erscheinungen bei der Erbauung der Gemeinde." *Communio Viatorum* 16 (Summer 1973): 147–62.

Geffcken, Johannes. *Komposition und Entstehungszeit der Oracula Sibyllina.* Leipzig: J. C. Hinrichs, 1902.

Gelpi, Donald D. *Charism and Sacrament: A Theology of Christian Conversion.* New York: Paulist, 1976.

Gnilka, Joachim. "Geistliches Amt und Gemeinde nach Paulus." In *Foi et Salut Selon S. Paul (Épître aux Romains 1:16).* In the Analecta Biblica, Vol. 42. Rome: Institut Biblique Pontifical, 1970.

Godet, F. *Commentary on St. Paul's Epistle to the Romans,* Vol. 1. Trans. A. Cusin. Edinburgh: T. & T. Clark, 1980.

Goldingay, John. *The Church and the Gifts of the Spirit.* Grove Booklets, No. 7. Bramcote, Notts.: n.p., 1972.

Goudge, H. L. *The First Epistle to the Corinthians.* In The Westminster Commentaries, ed. Walter Lock. London: Methuen & Co., 1903.

Green, Michael. *I Believe in the Holy Spirit.* Grand Rapids: Eerdmans, 1975.

Griffiths, Michael. *Grace-Gifts: Developing What God Has Given the Church.* Grand Rapids: Eerdmans, 1978.

Grosheide, F. W. *Commentary on the First Epistle to the Corinthians.* In the New International Commentary on the New Testament, ed. N. B. Stonehouse. Grand Rapids: Eerdmans, 1953.

Grossmann, Siegfried. *Charisma: The Gifts of the Spirit.* Transl. Susan Wiesmann. Wheaton, Ill.: Key Publishers, Inc., 1971.

Grudem, Wayne. "Response to Gerhard Dautzenberg on 1 Cor. 12:10." *Biblische Zeitschrift* 22 (7, 1978): 253–70.

———. *The Gift of Prophecy in 1 Corinthians.* Washington, D.C.: University Press of America, 1982.

Guthrie, Donald. *The Pastoral Epistles.* In The Tyndale New Testament Commentaries, Vol. 14, ed. R. V. G. Tasker. Grand Rapids: Eerdmans, 1957.

Hahn, Ferdinand. "Charisma und Amt: die Diskussion über das kirchliche Amt im Lichte der neutestamentlichen Charismenlehre." *Zeitschrift für Theologie und Kirche* 76 (1979): 419–49.

Hasenhüttl, Gotthold. *Charisma: Ordnungsprinzip der Kirche.* In Oekumenische Forschungen, Vol. 5, eds. Hans Küng and Josef Ratzinger. Freiburg: Verlag Herder KG, 1969.

Hill, David. *New Testament Prophecy.* Atlanta: John Knox, 1979.

Hollenweger, Walter J. *Conflict in Corinth and Memoirs of an Old Man. Two Stories That Illuminate the Way the Bible Came to be Written.* New York: Paulist, 1982.

———. "Creator Spiritus: The Challenge of Pentecostal Experience to Pentecostal Theology." *Theology* 81 (1, 1978): 32–40.

————. *The Pentecostals: The Charismatic Movement in the Churches.* Transl. R. A. Wilson. Minneapolis: Augsburg, 1972.

Holtz, Gottfried. *Die Pastoralbriefe.* In Theologischer Handkommentar zum Neuen Testament, Vol. 13, ed. D. Erich Fascher. Berlin: Evangelische Verlagsanstalt, 1965.

Holtz, Traugott. "Das Kennzeichen des Geistes: 1 Kor. 12:1–3." *New Testament Studies* 18 (4, 1972): 365–76.

Horton, Stanley M. *What the Bible Says About the Holy Spirit.* Springfield, Mo.: Gospel Publishing House, 1976.

Hurd, John Coolidge, Jr. *The Origin of 1 Corinthians.* New York: Seabury, 1965.

Käsemann, Ernst. *Commentary on Romans.* Transl. and ed. Geoffrey W. Bromiley. Grand Rapids: Eerdmans, 1980.

————. *Essays on New Testament Themes.* Transl. W. J. Montague. London: SCM, 1964.

Kee, Howard Clark. Preface to *Charismata: God's Gifts for God's People,* by John Koenig. Philadelphia: Westminster, 1978.

Kelly, John Norman Davidson. *A Commentary on the Pastoral Epistles (1 Timothy, 2 Timothy, Titus).* In Harper's New Testament Commentaries, ed. Henry Chadwick. New York: Harper & Row, 1963.

Kertelge, Karl. *Gemeinde und Amt im Neuen Testament.* Munich: Kösel-Verlag, 1972.

Kittel, Gerhard and G. Friedrich, eds. *Theological Dictionary of the New Testament,* 10 vols. Transl. Geoffrey W. Bromiley. Grand Rapids: Eerdmans, 1964–1976.

Knox, John. "The Epistle to the Romans: Introduction and Exegesis." In *The Interpreter's Bible,* Vol. 9, ed. George Arthur Buttrick. New York: Abingdon, 1954.

Koenig, John. *Charismata: God's Gifts for God's People.* In the Biblical Perspectives on Current Issues series, ed. Howard Clark Kee. Philadelphia: Westminster, 1978.

————. "From Mystery to Ministry: Paul as Interpreter of Charismatic Gifts." *Union Seminary Quarterly Review* 33 (Spring 1978): 167–74.

Küng, Hans. *Die Kirche.* Freiburg im Breisgau: Verlag Herder KG, 1967. (English: *The Church,* Image Books. Garden City, N.Y.: Doubleday & Co., Inc., 1976.)

Kydd, Ronald A. N. *Charismatic Gifts in the Early Church.* Peabody, Mass.: Hendrickson Publishers, Inc., 1984.

Laporte, Jean. "The Holy Spirit, Source of Life and Activity According to the Early Church." In *Perspectives on Charismatic Renewal,* ed. Edward D. O'Connor. Notre Dame: University of Notre Dame Press, 1975.

Laurentin, René. "Charisms: Terminological Precision." In *Charisms in the Church,* eds. Christian Duquoc and Casiano Floristan. In the series Concilium: Religion in the Seventies, Vol. 109. New York: Seabury, 1978.

Lemaire, André. "Ministries in the New Testament: Recent Research;" bibliographic essay, transl. from French. *Biblical Theology Bulletin* 3 (6, 1973): 133–66.

Lietzmann, D. Hans, and Werner Georg Kümmel. *An die Korinther I/II*, 5th ed. In Handbuch zum Neuen Testament, Vol. 9, ed. Günther Bornkamm. Tübingen: J. C. B. Mohr (Paul Siebeck), 1969.

Lohse, Eduard. "Die Gemeinde und ihre Ordnung bei den Synoptikern und bei Paulus." In *Jesus und Paulus*, eds. E. Earle Ellis and Erich Grässer. Göttingen: Vandenhoeck & Ruprecht, 1975.

Lock, Walter. *A Critical and Exegetical Commentary on the Pastoral Epistles*. In the International Critical Commentary, eds. Samuel Rolles Driver, Alfred Plummer, and Charles Augustus Briggs. Edinburgh: T. & T. Clark, 1924; reprint, 1966.

MacArthur, John. *The Charismatics: A Doctrinal Perspective*. Grand Rapids: Zondervan, 1978.

McDonnell, Kilian. *Charismatic Renewal and the Churches*. New York: Seabury, 1976.

———. "The Experience of the Holy Spirit in the Catholic Charismatic Renewal." In *Conflicts About the Holy Spirit*, eds. Hans Küng and Jürgen Moltmann. In the series Concilium: Religion in the Seventies, Vol. 128. New York: Seabury, 1979.

MacGorman, J. W. *Romans, 1 Corinthians*. In the Layman's Bible Book Commentary, Vol. 20. Nashville: Broadman, 1980.

———. *The Gifts of the Spirit*. Nashville: Broadman, 1974.

Moffatt, James. *The First Epistle of Paul to the Corinthians*. In The Moffatt New Testament Commentary, ed. James Moffatt. London: Hodder & Stoughton Ltd., 1938.

Moltmann, Jürgen. *The Church in the Power of the Spirit: A Contribution to Messianic Ecclesiology*. Transl. Margaret Kohl. New York: Harper & Row, 1977.

Moody, Dale. *The Word of Truth. A Summary of Christian Doctrine Based on Biblical Revelation*. Grand Rapids: Eerdmans, 1981.

Morris, Leon. *The First Epistle of Paul to the Corinthians: An Introduction and Commentary*. In The Tyndale New Testament Commentaries, Vol. 7, ed. R. V. G. Tasker. Grand Rapids: Eerdmans, 1958.

Mühlen, Heribert. "The Charismatic Renewal as Experience." In *The Holy Spirit and Power*, ed. Kilian McDonnell. Garden City, N.Y.: Doubleday & Co., Inc., 1975.

———. *A Charismatic Theology: Initiation in the Spirit*. Transl. Edward Quinn and Thomas Linton. New York: Paulist, 1978.

Müller, Ulrich B. *Prophetie und Predigt im Neuen Testament: Formgeschichtliche Untersuchungen zur urchristlichen Prophetie*. Gütersloh: Gütersloher Verlagshaus Gerd Mohn, 1975.

Murray, John. *The Epistle to the Romans*, 1 vol. ed. In the New International Commentary on the New Testament, ed. F. F. Bruce. Grand Rapids: Eerdmans, 1968.

Neill, Stephen. *The Interpretation of the New Testament 1861–1961*. London: Oxford University Press, 1964.

Nygren, Anders. *Commentary on Romans*. Transl. Carl C. Rasmussen. Philadelphia: Muhlenberg Press, 1949.

Orr, William F., and James Arthur Walther. *1 Corinthians*. In The Anchor Bible, eds. Frank M. Cross, Raymond E. Brown, and Jonas C. Greenfield. Garden City, N.Y.: Doubleday & Co., Inc., 1976.

Oudersluys, Richard C. "Charismatic Theology and the New Testament." *Reformed Review* 28 (Fall 1974): 48–59.

———. "The Purpose of Spiritual Gifts." *Reformed Review* 28 (Spring 1975): 212–22.

Parry, R. St. John. *The Epistle of Paul the Apostle to the Corinthians*. In the Cambridge Greek Testament for Schools and Colleges. Cambridge: Cambridge University Press, 1926.

———. *The Epistle of Paul the Apostle to the Romans*. In the Cambridge Greek Testament for Schools and Colleges. Cambridge: Cambridge University Press, 1921.

Piepkorn, Arthur Carl. "*Charisma* in the New Testament and the Apostolic Fathers." *Concordia Theological Monthly* 42 (6, 1971): 369–389.

Plummer, Alfred. *A Critical and Exegetical Commentary on the Second Epistle of St. Paul to the Corinthians*. In the International Critical Commentary, eds. Samuel Rolles Driver, Alfred Plummer, and Charles Augustus Briggs. Edinburgh: T. & T. Clark, 1915; reprint, 1966.

Priebe, Duane A. "Charismatic Gifts and Christian Existence in Paul." In *Gifts of the Spirit and the Body of Christ: Perspectives on the Charismatic Movement*, ed. J. Elmo Agrimson. Minneapolis: Augsburg, 1974.

Rahner, Karl. *Theological Investigations, Vol. XVI. Experience of the Spirit: Source of Theology*. Transl. David Morland. New York: Seabury, 1979.

———. *The Spirit in the Church*. Transl. John Griffiths. New York: Seabury, 1979.

Ratzinger, Joseph. "Bemerkungen zur Frage der Charismen in der Kirche." In *Die Zeit Jesu*, eds. Günther Bornkamm and Karl Rahner. Freiburg: Verlag Herder KG, 1970.

Richards, J. R. "Romans and 1 Corinthians: Their Chronological Relationship and Comparative Dates." *New Testament Studies* 13 (10, 1966): 14–30.

Robertson, Archibald, and Alfred Plummer. *A Critical and Exegetical Commentary on the First Epistle of St. Paul to the Corinthians*, 2nd ed. In the International Critical Commentary, eds. Samuel Rolles Driver, Alfred Plummer, and Charles Augustus Briggs. Edinburgh: T. & T. Clark, 1914; reprint, 1963.

Robinson, D. W. B. "Charismata versus Pneumatika; Paul's Method of Discussion." *The Reformed Theological Review* 31 (5, 1972): 49–55.

Ruef, John. *Paul's First Letter to Corinth*. In the Westminster Pelican Commentaries, ed. D. E. Nineham. Philadelphia: Westminster, 1977.

Saake, Helmut. "Pneumatologia Paulina; zur Katholizität der Problematik des Charisma." *Catholica* 26 (7, 1972): 212–23.

Sanday, William, and Arthur C. Headlam. *A Critical and Exegetical Commentary on the Epistle to the Romans*, 5th ed. In the International Critical Commentary, eds. Samuel Rolles Driver, Alfred Plummer, and Charles Augustus Briggs. Edinburgh: T. & T. Clark, 1902.

Satake, Akira. "Apostolat und Gnade bei Paulus." *New Testament Studies* 15

(1968–69): 96–105.

Schlier, Heinrich. *Der Römerbrief.* In Herders Theologischer Kommentar zum Neuen Testament, Vol. 6, eds. Alfred Wikenhauser, Anton Vögtle, and Rudolf Schnackenburg. Freiburg: Verlag Herder, 1977.

————. "Herkunft, Ankunft und Wirkungen des Heiligen Geistes im Neuen Testament." In *Erfahrung und Theologie des Heiligen Geistes*, eds. Claus Heitmann and Heribert Mühlen. Hamburg: Kösel-Verlag, 1974.

Schmidt, Hans Wilhelm. *Der Brief des Paulus an die Römer.* In Theologischer Handkommentar zum Neuen Testament, Vol. 6, ed. E. Erich Fascher. Berlin: Evangelische Verlagsanstalt, 1962.

Schmithals, Walter. *Die Gnosis in Korinth.* Göttingen: Vandenhoeck & Ruprecht, 1969. (English: *Gnosticism in Corinth: An Investigation of the Letters to the Corinthians.* Transl. John Steely. Nashville: Abingdon, 1971.)

————. "Geisterfahrung als Christuserfahrung." In *Erfahrung und Theologie des Heiligen Geistes*, eds. Claus Heitmann and Heribert Mühlen. Hamburg: Agentur des Rauhen Hauses, and Munich: Kösel-Verlag, 1974.

Schulz, Siegfried. "Die Charismenlehre des Paulus: Bilanz der Probleme und Ergebnisse." In *Rechtfertigung*, eds. Johannes Friedrich, Wolfgang Pöhlmann, and Peter Stuhlmacher. Tübingen: J. C. B. Mohr, and Göttingen: Vandenhoeck & Ruprecht, 1976.

Schürmann, Heinz. "Die Geistlichen Gnadengaben in den paulinischen Gemeinden." In *Ursprung und Gestalt: Erörterungen und Besinnungen zum Neuen Testament.* Düsseldorf: Patmos-Verlag, 1970.

Schütz, John Howard. "Charisma and Social Reality in Primitive Christianity." *The Journal of Religion* 54 (1, 1974): 51–70.

————. *Paul and the Anatomy of Apostolic Authority.* In the Society for New Testament Studies Monograph Series, Vol. 26, ed. Matthew Black. Cambridge: Cambridge University Press, 1975.

Schweizer, Eduard. *The Holy Spirit.* Transl. Reginald H. and Ilse Fuller. Philadelphia: Fortress Press, 1980.

————. "What is the Holy Spirit: A Study in Biblical Theology." Transl. G. W. S. Knowles. In *Conflicts About the Holy Spirit*, eds. Hans Küng and Jürgen Moltmann. In the series Concilium: Religion in the Seventies, Vol. 128. New York: Seabury, 1979.

Serr, Jacques. "Les charismes dans la vie de l'église; temoignages patristiques." *Foi et Vie* 72 (1973): 33–42.

Smail, Thomas A. *Reflected Glory: The Spirit in Christ and Christians.* Grand Rapids: Eerdmans, 1975.

Spicq, P. C. *Saint Paul: Les Épîtres Pastorales.* In Études Bibliques. Paris: Librairie Lecoffre, 1947.

Stagg, Frank. *The Book of Acts. The Early Struggle for an Unhindered Gospel.* Nashville: Broadman, 1955.

Stendahl, Krister. "Glossolalia: The New Testament Evidence." In *Paul Among Jews and Gentiles.* Philadelphia: Fortress, 1976; reprinted from *The Charismatic Movement*, ed. Michael P. Hamilton. Grand Rapids: Eerdmans, 1975.

Taylor, John V. *The Go-Between God: The Holy Spirit and the Christian Mission.* Philadelphia: Fortress, 1973.

Theissen, Gerd. *The Social Setting of Pauline Christianity: Essays on Corinth.* Ed., transl., and with an introduction by John H. Schütz. Philadelphia: Fortress, 1982.

Therrien, Gérard. *Le Discernement dans les Écrits Pauliniens.* In Études Bibliques. Paris: Librairie Lecoffre, 1973.

Thiselton, Anthony C. "The 'Interpretation' of Tongues: a New Suggestion in the Light of Greek Usage in Philo and Josephus." *Journal of Theological Studies*, n.s., 30 (4, 1979): 15–36.

Von Campenhausen, Hans Freiherr. *Kirchliches Amt und geistliche Vollmacht in den ersten drei Jahrhunderten.* In Beiträge zur Historischen Theologie, Vol. 14, ed. Gerhard Ebeling. Tübingen: J. C. B. Mohr (Paul Siebeck), 1953. (English: *Ecclesiastical Authority and Spiritual Power in the Church of the First Three Centuries.* Transl. J. A. Baker. Stanford: Stanford University Press, 1969.)

Waalvoord, John F. "Contemporary Issues in the Doctrine of the Holy Spirit. IV, Spiritual Gifts Today." *Bibliotheca Sacra* 130 (10, 1973): 315–28.

Weber, Max. *Economy and Society: An Outline of Interpretive Sociology*, 3 vols. Ed. Guenther Roth and Claus Wittich. Transl. Ephraim Fischoff et al. New York: Bedminster Press, 1968.

——. *Gesammelte Aufsätze zur Religionssoziologie*, 3 vols., 5th ed. Vol. 1: *Die Wirtschaftsethik der Weltreligionen.* Tübingen: J. C. B. Mohr (Paul Siebeck), 1963.

Wendland, Heinz-Dietrich. *Die Briefe an die Korinther*, 8th ed. In Das Neue Testament Deutsch, eds. Paul Althaus and Gerhard Friedrich. Göttingen: Vandenhoeck & Ruprecht, 1962.

Williams, J. Rodman. *The Pentecostal Reality.* Plainfield, N.J.: Logos International, 1972.

Windisch, Hans. *Der zweite Korintherbrief*, 9th ed. Republished and ed. Georg Stracker. Göttingen: Vandenhoeck & Ruprecht, 1970.

Index of Authors

Alciphron, 3, 52
Allo, P. E.-B., 33, 59
Agrimson, J. E., 91
Baker, D. L., 59, 78, 82
Baker, J. A., 81, 91
Banks, R., 12, 36, 60–62, 69, 75, 78–79, 81–82, 92–93, 100
Barrett, C. K., 23, 27, 31, 45, 48, 52–57, 59, 61–64
Bartling, W. J., 31, 57, 59, 67, 80, 87, 93
Baur, F. C., 8–9, 13
Behm, J., 62
Betz, O., 96, 100
Beyer, H. W., 55
Bittlinger, A., 8, 13, 73–74, 81
Black, M., 52–53
Bonnetain, S. P., 11
Bouchet, J.-R., 76, 82
Brandt, R. L., 60
Bridge, D., 62
Brockhaus, U., 12, 18, 33, 46, 52–54, 57–60, 62–64, 84, 92
Brown, R. P., 62, 78, 82
Bruce, F. F., 53, 58–60, 62–64
Bühlmann, W., 93
Bultmann, R., 2, 11–12, 54, 64
Campenhausen, von H. F., 61, 70, 81, 84, 97, 100
Conzelmann, H., 11, 27, 34, 37, 57–61, 64, 82, 92
Corley, B., 53
Cranfield, C. E. B., 52–53
Cullmann, O., 47, 62–63
Culpepper, R. H., 54, 82, 93
Daines, B., 63
Dautzenberg, G., 40–41, 61–62
deBoor, W., 64

Delling, G., 63
Denney, J., 52
Dibelius, M., 64–65
Dodd, C. H., 53
Doughty, D. J., 11–12, 81
Dunn, J. D. G., 4, 8, 10–13, 24, 41, 46, 48, 53–56, 59–64, 71–72, 74–75, 81–82, 84, 92, 98, 100
Ellis, E. E., 7, 13, 39, 58–59, 61, 89, 93
Eichholz, G., 74, 81
Fee, G. D., 64
Findlay, G. G., 57–59
Foerster, W., 100
Fowler, S., 80, 92
Fraikin, D., 14, 52, 82
Friedrich, G., 21, 54
Fung, R. Y. K., 93
Gábrïs, K., 49, 64, 73, 81, 96, 100
Geffcken, J., 12
Gelpi, D. L., 67, 80
Gnilka, J., 19, 54
Godet, F., 52
Goldingay, J., 8, 13
Goudge, H. L., 58
Green, M., 54, 60, 62
Griffiths, J., 81, 93
Grosheide, F. W., 57, 60
Grossmann, S., 55, 61–62
Grudem, W., 61–62
Guthrie, D., 64
Hasenhüttl, G., 10–11, 13, 15, 29, 37, 52–55, 57–58, 60–61, 63–65, 69–70, 76, 81–82, 86, 92, 100
Hahn, F., 91–92

Headlam, A. C., 54–56
Heidland, H. W., 53
Hill, D., 22, 54–55, 61
Hollenweger, W. J., 12–13, 31, 42,
    57, 59, 62, 81–82, 87–89, 93
Holtz, G., 64
Holtz, T., 33, 59, 63
Horton, S., 61
Hurd, J. C. Jr., 57–58, 62
Josephus, 3, 40, 43
Käsemann, E., 8, 11–13, 16–17,
    52–56, 59, 63, 67, 75–76, 80,
    82, 84–85, 92, 97, 100
Kee, H. C., 13
Kelly, J. N. D., 64
Kertelge, K., 53–54, 61
Knox, J., 56
Koenig, J., 6, 10–13, 53, 56, 71,
    76, 81–82, 93
Kümmel, W. G., 58
Küng, H., 86, 92
Kydd, R. A. N., 12
LaPorte, J., 82
LaPotterrie, de, I., 11
Laurentin, R., 73, 81
Lemaire, A., 100
Lietzmann, H., 34, 58, 60, 62, 64
Lock, W., 64–65
Lohse, E., 63
McDonnell, K., 68, 81, 86, 92
MacArthur, J., 30, 58
MacGorman, J. W., 28, 57–58,
    60–63, 74, 81
Moffatt, J., 44, 63
Moltmann, J., 13, 28, 53, 57–58,
    75, 82, 85, 92–93
Moody, D., 63
Morris, L., 57, 59
Mühlen, H., 85–86, 92
Müller, U. B., 39, 54, 61–62
Murray, J., 52–56
Neill, S., 11
Nygren, A., 52
Orr, W. F., 57, 60
Oudersluys, R. C., 13, 34, 52,
    57–58, 60, 82, 93

Parry, R. St. John., 52–53, 56, 60
Philo, 3, 40, 42–43
Phypers, D., 62
Piepkorn, A. C., 12, 53, 64, 100
Plummer, A., 57, 59, 64
Priebe, D., 8, 13, 57, 63
Rahner, K., 9, 13, 85–86, 92
Ratzinger, J., 61
Rengstorf, K. H., 63
Richards, J. R., 12
Robertson, A., 57, 59
Robinson, D. W. B., 6, 59
Ruef, J., 32, 57, 59, 62
Saake, H., 59
Sanday, W., 54–56
Satake, A., 100
Schlier, H., 54–56, 60
Schmidt, H. W., 52–53
Schmithals, W., 30, 58
Schmitz, O., 25, 55–56
Schneider, J., 63
Schulz, S., 3, 8, 11–13, 83,
    91–92, 100
Schürmann, H., 34, 36, 54–55,
    60, 79, 82, 90, 93
Schütz, J. H., 68, 80, 95–96, 100
Schweizer, E., 12, 59, 70, 81–82,
    84, 89, 93
Serr, J., 82
Sister Evangéline, 58
Smail, T. A., 68, 81–82
Spicq, P. C., 65
Stagg, F., 64
Stendahl, K., 60
Stephanou, E. A., 82
Taylor, J. V., 102
Theissen, G., 59
Thérrien, G., 62
Thiselton, A. G., 43, 62
Waalvoord, J. F., 82
Walther, J. A., 57, 60
Weber, M., 1, 11, 94–96, 100
Wendland, H. D., 57–59, 61–62,
    64
Williams, J. R., 17, 53
Windisch, H., 64

Index of Scripture References

Gen 32:19   44
Ps 30:22   3
    31:22   11
Prov 22:8   26
Mt 22:25   44
Jn 16:7–10   89
    16:8–11   91
Acts 2:4   62
    2:5–13   93
    2:8   93
    2:11   93
    3:14   53
    6:6   49
    13:3   49
    14:8–10   79
    16:16–30   79
    19:11–12   79
    19:23–41   48
    27:11   45
Acts 28:1–6   79
    28:8–9   79
Rom 1:11   4–5, 7, 12, 14–15,
21, 51
    1:12   15
    3:24   2
    5:5   48
    5:15   2, 4–6, 15–18, 50,
52
    5:15–17   16
    5:16   2, 4–6, 15–18, 50,
52
    5:17   17, 52
    6:23   2, 4–5, 17–18, 50
    8:9–17   89
    8:32   18, 53
    9:4   18
    9–11   18

11:13   22
11:26   53
11:28   18
11:29   4–5, 13, 18–19,
51
    12   54, 73
    12–15   24
    12:1   24
    12:1–2   77
    12:3   19, 85
    12:3–8   19
    12:5   20
    12:6   4, 12, 15, 20–21,
38, 53
    12:6–8   5, 19–21, 26,
35, 44, 48, 50–51, 55, 63, 67,
69, 72–73, 84, 91, 96
    12:7   20, 23, 53, 67
    12:8   20, 25, 45, 53,
55–56
    12:14–15   89
    15:9   38
    15:22   23
    15:25–31   23
1 Cor 1–3   36
    1:1   44
    1:5   26–27
    1:7   4–5, 26–28, 51, 57
    1:10   27
    1:10–4:21   30
    1:11   30
    1:12   28, 36, 42
    1:18–25   36
    2:12   53
    2:13   32
    2:13–14   31
    3:1   31

3:10   44
5:1−5   100
5:1−13   30
6:1−11   30
6:12−20   30
7   29−30
7:1   28
7:7   4−5, 28−29, 51
7:26   29
7:29−31   29
8:1   36
8:1−11:1   30
9:11   31
11   58
11:2−34   30
11:4−5   61
12   15, 29, 31, 34−35, 38, 44−45, 47−48, 51, 72, 87, 96
12−14   5−7, 15, 19, 21−22, 27, 29−48, 30−31, 35, 39−42, 48, 50, 57, 61, 67, 72, 93, 96, 99
12:1   6, 24, 31−32, 34−35, 39
12:1−3   29, 31−34, 60
12:1−14:40   30
12:2   32−33, 42, 93
12:3   31, 33, 41−42, 93, 99, 103
12:4   4, 32, 34−35, 42, 60, 74
12:4−6   6, 29, 34−35
12:4−11   46, 60
12:5   22, 60, 70, 100
12:5−7   86
12:6   60, 71
12:7   22, 35, 68, 71, 85, 89
12:7−11   60
12:8   35−36, 78
12:8−10   5, 19−20, 27, 30, 35−43, 57, 59−60, 69, 72
12:9   4, 37, 50
12:9−10   78
12:10   38, 41, 93
12:11   22, 68, 72, 78−79,

86, 89
12:12   71
12:12−27   19, 30, 35, 43, 45−47, 60, 68, 70, 79
12:13   46
12:14−20   46, 63
12:14−27   46
12:18   46, 71
12:21−26   46, 63, 85
12:24   71
12:28   4, 20, 23, 30, 35, 37−39, 43−45, 50, 60, 69, 71, 84−86, 96, 98
12:28−30   19, 24, 46, 60, 86
12:29   39
12:29−30   30, 35, 43, 69
12:29−31   45
12:30   4, 37, 50
12:31   4, 7, 31, 47, 79
13   27, 30, 47−48, 58, 78
13:1−3   35
13:2   36−37, 62
13:3   56
13:4−7   41
13:8   36, 78
13:8−9   77
13:10   47, 78
13:12   40
14   38, 40, 42−43, 58−59, 88
14:1   6−7, 32, 39, 47, 59, 79
14:1−6   40
14:2   43
14:3   20−21, 24−25, 39, 55
14:3−25   40
14:4   43
14:5   38, 43, 59
14:5−12   43
14:6   35, 59
14:13   59
14:16−17   43
14:18   43
14:19   43
14:24−25   39, 88

14:26   35, 43, 59, 71
14:26–28   59
14:26–33   41
14:28   43
14:29   40, 62, 98
14:31   22, 38
14:32   42
14:33   22
14:37   31
14:37–40   41
14:39   22
15:1–58   30
15:7–9   44
15:10   12
15:46   31
16:1   30
16:12   30
16:15   23
16:17   30
2 Cor 1:3–7   25
1:8–11   48
1:11   4–5, 48–49, 51
1:24   98
2:7   2, 53
2:10   2, 53, 100
4:1   22
5:18   22
8:2   25
8:4   23
8:6–7   56
8:19   56
9:1   23
9:7   26
9:11–13   25
9:12–13   23
9:15   17, 53
10:1   55

10:6   100
12:9   12
12:13   2, 53
Gal 1:1   98
1:23   54
3:18   2
Eph 2:5   2
2:8   2, 6
2:20   23
3:7   85
4:1   55
4:7   6, 16
4:7–12   67
4:8   6
4:11   19–20, 24, 44, 84,
88, 90
4:11–12   66
4:12   20, 22
4:32   2, 53
Phil 4:2   55
Col 2:13   53
3:13   53
3:16   55
1 Thes 1:3   22
4:1   55
5:12   26
5:20   41
5:21   41, 62, 98
1 Tim 3:4   26
4:14   4–5, 49–50, 51,
64, 84
4:20   79
2 Tim 1:6   4–5, 49–50, 51,
64, 84
Jas 1:17   52
1 Pet 4:10   4, 54
Rev 18:17   45